MINISTER TO OTHERS

RICHARD LEACH
and DAVID A. WHEELER

LifeWay Press®
Nashville, Tennessee

ISBN 978-1-4158-6639-9
Item 005085769

Dewey decimal classification: 259
Subject headings: WITNESSING \ MINISTRY \ INTERPERSONAL RELATIONS

Cover illustration: Mac Premo

All Scripture quotations are taken from the Holman Christian Standard Bible®,
copyright © 1999, 2000, 2002, 2003 by Holman Bible Publishers.

To order additional copies of this resource, write to LifeWay Church Resources
Customer Service; One LifeWay Plaza; Nashville, TN 37234-0113; fax (615) 251-5933;
phone toll free (800) 458-2772; order online at *www.lifeway.com;*
e-mail *orderentry@lifeway.com;* or visit the LifeWay Christian Store serving you.

Printed in the United States of America

Leadership and Adult Publishing
LifeWay Church Resources
One LifeWay Plaza
Nashville, TN 37234-0175

Contents

Introducing Richard Leach & David A. Wheeler

Richard Leach leads the servant and ministry-evangelism team at the North American Mission Board of the Southern Baptist Convention. This team helps churches network for evangelism; gather new believers in small groups that can become new churches; and develop leaders through the use of servant and ministry-evangelism resources, processes, and products.

Richard is also the chief executive officer of New Orleans Baptist Ministries Inc., a corporation that assists churches in reaching New Orleans with the gospel, that provides Southern Baptists opportunities to experience ministry evangelism, and that offers opportunities for evangelism research and development in an urban setting.

Richard holds a bachelor of science and a master of business administration from Louisiana Tech University, a master of divinity from Southwestern Baptist Theological Seminary, and a doctor of ministry from Mid-America Baptist Theological Seminary.

David A. Wheeler is a professor of evangelism at Liberty Baptist Theological Seminary and Liberty University. He also represents the North American Mission Board as a field missionary on campus, where he serves as the associate director of the church-planting center and the ministry-training center and as the director of applied ministries.

David often leads conferences on servant ministries for churches and Baptist state conventions. David frequently contributes articles on creative evangelistic approaches to *SBCLife* and *OnMission* magazines. He is the author of *Servanthood Evangelism Manual* and a contributor to *Ministry Evangelism Tool Kit, Total Church Life Workbook, Prayer to Share Material, Praying Your Friends to Christ, Family to Family,* and *Evangelism Planner.*

David holds a bachelor in science from Tennessee Tech University and a master of divinity and a doctor of philosophy from Southwestern Baptist Theological Seminary.

Introducing Minister to Others

Churches today are discovering that they can increase their relevancy to their communities by building relational bridges through which they can meet needs and intentionally share the gospel. In fact, "service-oriented evangelistic ministries are among the purest expressions of ministry-based evangelism available to the church in the new millennium. ... As a basic expression of ministry-based evangelism, many people have discovered new joy in witnessing through a tool known as 'servanthood evangelism.' "[1]

That statement recognizes that ministry requires something of the person providing ministry to others. This resource will take you on a journey to develop what true ministry requires of the one who acts—a servant lifestyle.

Five principles provide a foundation for linking evangelism to acts of ministry:
1. Ministry should be seen as an incarnation of the gospel.
2. Ministry should be a vehicle for spiritual transformation.
3. Ministry should extend to every individual.
4. Ministry is best communicated through servants who live servant lifestyles.
5. Ministry will cost you something.[2]

Let's start by thinking about the gifts God has given you. They are not solely for your benefit. God makes a provision, described as "the gift" in 1 Peter 4:10, and deposits it in you: "Based on the gift they have received, everyone should use it to serve others, as good managers of the varied grace of God." As a matter of fact, God makes lots of deposits in you—things like time, money, abilities, possessions, influence, and relationships. In 1 Peter 4:10 the article *the* is absent in the Greek, so it implies any provision given by the Holy Spirit. Any time you can benefit someone, regard what you have and what they don't have as an opportunity for ministry that God has given you.

True ministry to others, ministry that was modeled by Jesus Christ, requires you to minister as a servant. A servant recognizes that, as a possessor of resources, he is a steward of what he possesses. Said another way, serving is more than just an act. It is an attitude about yourself, the one you serve, and the thing you give away. It even requires your heart to be behind the act of ministry (see Proverbs 23:6-8). That's why serving is often called an act of kindness. You do it for someone else's benefit, not your own.

What would life be like for you if you used your assets to serve others in your neighborhood, in your community, or in your sphere of influence? Remember, that's exactly what 1 Peter 4:10 says God requires you to do. What if your church used its resources to serve the community?

Perhaps this is a good place for you to start your study of *Minister to Others*. What is the level of your concern for others? After reading the four statements below, check the response that most accurately describes you.

○ I place high value on my neighbors.
○ I have a healthy concern for my neighbors.
○ I frequently think about my neighbors.
○ I respond to the needs of my neighbors when prompted to do so.

How did you do? Proverbs 23:7 says that as a person thinks in his heart, so is he. In other words, changing your idea about people will lead you to change your actions toward them. Do you have a servant inside you? You do if you have trusted in Jesus as your Savior and Lord. A servant is there because Jesus lives inside you, and He is the greatest Servant of all time!

Minister to Others will help you become the servant God created you to be when Jesus came to dwell in your heart. Through this study you will—

• identify ministry actions that will connect you with God's activity around you;
• surrender to a lifestyle of servanthood;
• identify barriers to servanthood;
• learn how to assess and meet needs;
• recognize the importance of connecting acts of ministry with the good news;
• discover ways to network with others to expand your ministry reach;
• explain why abiding in Christ is essential to ministry;
• define what it means to be a neighbor to someone in need;
• learn principles for announcing the coming of God's kingdom;
• state why self-denial is key to sacrificial service;
• identify ways you can pass the baton of service to others.

SMALL-GROUP STUDY OF *MINISTER TO OTHERS*

Although you could study this book alone, we want you to experience God's best. When God saved you, He placed you in the body of Christ so that you can benefit from the ministry of other members of the body. You are also in the body to help others. I encourage you to join a group of other believers in Christ and work through this study together. Group members can help one another live the truths of the study.

If you are the person who will lead the small-group sessions, we've included a brief leader guide, beginning on page 108. A guide for each small-group session appears at the end of each week's daily devotionals so that all group members will have access to the questions and sharing activities.

PERSONAL STUDY OF *MINISTER TO OTHERS*

This book may be different from others you have read. This is a self-paced, interactive study. We are not just speaking to you as we write. We want you to interact with us and with the Lord, so we will give you instructions for at least two types of activities.

One is a prayer activity that begins with an arrow pointing up to God and down to you. The arrow symbolizes what we want you to do in prayer: talk to the Lord and listen as He speaks to you.

The other kind of activity will begin with a circled number. In these learning activities we may ask you a question and give you instructions for responding. Or we may give you instructions about a ministry action we want you to take. Take these learning activities seriously. They will help you understand and apply the truths to your life.

Each week you will study five daily lessons before meeting with a mentor or a small group to process what you are learning. Don't wait until the end of the week to start your study. We don't want you to be overwhelmed by having too much to do in too short a time. But more importantly, we want you to develop a habit of spending time with God every day. Take time every day to read God's Word, study or meditate on its meaning, and talk to God in prayer. For the next six weeks let this book be your guide. You will need to study week 1 before your first small-group session.

We also want you to memorize Bible verses about being a servant of Christ. We've chosen a verse or verses for each week that apply to the topic for the week.

Turn to the back of the book and tear out the Scirpture-memory cards. Use one each week to memorize the assigned verse(s) and review the verses from previous weeks.

1. Jerry Pipes et al., *His Heart, Our Hands: Ministry Evangelism as a Tool for Church Planting* [online], n.d. [cited 7 October 2008], 16. Available from the Internet: *www.churchplantingvillage.net.*
2. Ibid., 5–6.

Week 1

Connecting with God's Activity Around You

"Based on the gift they have received, everyone should use it to serve others, as good managers of the varied grace of God."

1 Peter 4:10

Connecting with God's Activity Around You

This week's study will expand your concept of ministry to others. In giving you eternal life, Jesus made provision for you to join Him in what He is doing in this world. He equipped you by giving you abilities, strength, opportunities, experiences, relationships, and resources—all for the sole purpose of making His gift available to others. Putting those assets to use, whatever they are, creates opportunities for you to minister to others—both lost persons and fellow believers. The resources God has given you are not for your benefit but for the benefit of others. This week you will explore some ways you can start reaching out to serve others with the love of Christ.

LEARNING GOAL
By observing ministry roles in Scripture and through personal observation, you will identify ministry actions that will connect you with God's activity around you.

OVERVIEW OF WEEK 1
Day 1: Watch a Bridge Builder
Day 2: Watch a Reliever
Day 3: Watch an Intercessor
Day 4: Watch an Encourager
Day 5: Watch a Personal Trainer

VERSE TO MEMORIZE
1 Peter 4:10

DISCIPLESHIP HELPS FOR WEEK 1
My Ministry List (p. 92)
Profile of a Servant Lifestyle (p. 93)

Day 1 • Watch a Bridge Builder

God's Word for Today

"*17If anyone is in Christ, there is a new creation; old things have passed away, and look, new things have come. 18Now everything is from God, who reconciled us to Himself through Christ and gave us the ministry of reconciliation: 19that is, in Christ, God was reconciling the world to Himself, not counting their trespasses against them, and He has committed the message of reconciliation to us. 20Therefore, we are ambassadors for Christ; certain that God is appealing through us, we plead on Christ's behalf, 'Be reconciled to God.' 21He made the One who did not know sin to be sin for us, so that we might become the righteousness of God in Him.*"

2 Corinthian 5:17-21

↕ **Read and meditate on "God's Word for Today" in the margin and spend a moment in prayer as you begin today's lesson.**

Individuals who have put their trust in Jesus Christ face an obstacle in relating to lost people, because a great divide exists between believers and unbelievers. Christians who want to be bridge builders understand that separation, as well as the process required for lost persons to come to faith in Jesus Christ. Bridge building involves changing an individual's receptivity to the gospel and developing the individual's ability to trust.

It's all about a relationship. Receptivity grows as the lost person observes the impact of the gospel in the life of someone he or she trusts. Every believer in Christ has an assignment to pass this trust on to others. The Bible calls that assignment the ministry of reconciliation. The love of Christ, demonstrated in word and deed, is never complete without the introduction of the gospel. No act of serving is complete until a Christian servant connects his intentional acts of kindness with the gospel.

One of the greatest challenges every follower of Jesus Christ faces is moving ministry actions, conversations, and relationships to a spiritual level to introduce the person's need for Christ. In his second letter to the church in Corinth, Paul tried to communicate to a group of new Christians, who were living in a highly immoral culture, the assignment that was theirs because of their relationship with Jesus Christ.

1️⃣ **Review "God's Word for Today" in the margin. What did Paul say is our ministry of reconciliation (see v. 18)?**

_____

What is our message of reconciliation (see v. 19)?

_____

Paul said we have both the *ministry* of reconciliation and the *message* of reconciliation. As a result ("therefore," v. 20), Jesus Christ changes our conversation; and He pleads with our family, friends, and acquaintances through what we say.

(2) **Who does Paul say has been given the ministry of reconciliation?**

_____

Paul said he was "certain that God is appealing through us" (v. 20).

(3) **In your opinion, how might a believer come to the certainty Paul had?**

_____

_____

Because of his certainty, Paul said, "We plead on Christ's behalf, 'Be reconciled to God' " (v. 20).

(4) **Have you ever pleaded with someone? What was the reason for your intense effort to persuade?**

_____

You no doubt pleaded with someone because of the urgency and importance of a particular situation. Can there be a need more urgent and important than being reconciled with God?

(5) **This week you will be asked to observe people who are ministering to others. Each day suggests a number of actions you can choose from. Don't feel that you have to do them all. Choose several over the course of the week that are best suited to your schedule and your interests.**

Today make plans to observe someone who is introducing another person to Jesus Christ. Use "My Observation Journal" in the margin to record what you learned, felt, and decided to do as result of your experience. Choose one or more of the following actions.
- Ask a close friend, a Bible study leader, or a pastor in your church to let you join them when visiting a person to whom they will extend the message of reconciliation.
- Visit the Web site _www.mostimportantthing.org_ and read the testimony of an individual committed to reconciling others.
- Watch a television program in which a pastor preaches the gospel and extends an invitation to be reconciled to God through Jesus Christ.

(6) **Begin memorizing this week's memory verse, 1 Peter 4:10. If you would like, tear out and use the card at the back of the book.**

Receptivity grows as the lost person observes the impact of the gospel in the life of someone he or she trusts.

My Observation Journal

Watch and Pray
Pray about your desire to be an ambassador for Christ. Begin praying for lost persons you know and for opportunities to serve them and to share Christ with them.

Day 2 • Watch a Reliever

God's Word for Today

"Soon afterward He was on His way to a town called Nain. His disciples and a large crowd were traveling with Him. Just as He neared the gate of the town, a dead man was being carried out. He was his mother's only son, and she was a widow. A large crowd from the city was also with her. When the Lord saw her, He had compassion on her and said, 'Don't cry.' Then He came up and touched the open coffin, and the pallbearers stopped. And He said, 'Young man, I tell you, get up!' The dead man sat up and began to speak, and Jesus gave him to his mother. Then fear came over everyone, and they glorified God, saying, 'A great prophet has risen among us,' and 'God has visited His people.' This report about Him went throughout Judea and all the vicinity." Luke 7:11-17

↕ **Read and meditate on "God's Word for Today" in the margin and spend a moment in prayer as you begin today's lesson.**

In baseball a relief pitcher is a welcome sight to a starting pitcher who has "lost his stuff" or whose arm is hurting. A reliever in baseball does just what his title implies—he brings immediate relief!

Our memory verse for this week, 1 Peter 4:10, introduced us to the fact that God equips every believer to contribute to the welfare of others in numerous ways. Those abilities constitute ministry assignments. Helping others is the action we most often associate with ministry to others, so we readily recognize the need to bring relief to others in the traffic patterns of life.

As a matter of fact, the New Testament accounts of Jesus' life are filled with one relief-providing encounter after another. In Luke 7 Jesus' ministry was spontaneous; He was presented with an opportunity to bring immediate relief. On other occasions, as in the case when four friends lowered their friend on a pallet through the roof of a home to put him at the feet of Christ (see Luke 5:19), ministry was planned and intentional; but the result was the same. Their actions were designed to bring immediate relief.

1 **Read Luke 5:17-20 and refer to "God's Word for Today" in the margin. Based on these two accounts, answer the following questions.**

What type of relief did the mother receive? _____

_____

What relief did the lame man receive? _____

_____

What was Jesus' underlying motivation to provide relief?

_____

_____

What was the four friends' underlying motivation to seek relief for their friend?

_____

What hindrances were faced by the people who brought relief?

_____

_____

What resources were used by the people who brought relief?

_____

_____

From these accounts, list some identifying marks of someone who brings relief.

_____

_____

_____

What about your world? You may meet an individual who is agonizing over the death of a close family member. Perhaps you will encounter an individual who is looking for ways to assist a disabled friend. Maybe you have a close family member or a friend who is at the point of death or whose body or mind will not function in a way that allows him to integrate completely in everyday life.

2) **Identify someone in your life who needs immediate relief. Write the person's name on "My Ministry List," page 92. You will add others to this list throughout the study as you identify needs and minister.**

3) **Today make plans to observe people who display an awareness of and a response to opportunities to bring relief—people who are helping others. A pregnancy resource center, a clothes closet, or a food ministry is a great place to see relief at work; but relief can also be a simple act like opening a door for someone. Complete "My Observation Journal" in the margin, recording what you saw, what you felt, and what opportunities you had to help someone.**

4) **Quote this week's memory verse, 1 Peter 4:10, to a family member or a friend.**

Helping others is the action we most often associate with ministry to others.

My Observation Journal

Watch and Pray
Pray for the person you identified who needs relief. Ask God whether He wants you to do something to help and what He wants you to do.

Day 3 • Watch an Intercessor

God's Word for Today

"¹The words of Nehemiah son of Hacaliah: During the month of Chislev in the twentieth year, when I was in the fortress city of Susa, ²Hanani, one of my brothers, arrived with men from Judah, and I questioned them about Jerusalem and the Jewish remnant that had returned from exile. ³They said to me, 'The survivors in the province, who returned from the exile, are in great trouble and disgrace. Jerusalem's wall has been broken down, and its gates have been burned down.' ⁴When I heard these words, I sat down and wept. I mourned for a number of days, fasting and praying before the God of heaven. ⁵I said, 'LORD God of heaven, the great and awe-inspiring God who keeps His gracious covenant with those who love Him and keep His commands, ⁶let Your eyes be open and Your ears be attentive to hear Your servant's prayer that I now pray to You day and night for Your servants, the Israelites. I confess the sins we have committed against You. Both I and my father's house have sinned. ⁷We have acted corruptly toward You and have not kept the commands, statutes,

Read and meditate on "God's Word for Today" in the margin and spend a moment in prayer as you begin today's lesson.

In the weeks prior to writing this lesson, I (Richard) was reminded of the importance of having people who pray for you. My wife walked into the garage in tears. One of our sons-in-law had just called to tell us that our 10-year-old special-needs granddaughter had been run over by a car and was being flown to a children's hospital in Saint Louis. We stopped to pray, asking God to intervene and seeking His direction about what to do. God immediately led us to call people and ask them to pray for Him to intervene. They ministered to us by praying. Two hours later, we received word that, other than scrapes, bruises, and swelling in her leg, our granddaughter was fine. She had no broken bones and no internal injuries!

You can imagine the rejoicing that took place as we made a return phone call to everyone we had asked to pray. We recognized that our friends had ministered to us through their willingness to pray. Today you will see that sometimes God initiates prayer on behalf of something He wants to do. When the answer comes, God receives glory for it. Every day you have the opportunity to serve someone through the ministry of intercessory prayer.

Nehemiah's prayer in "God's Word for Today" provides a helpful model for believers who want to minister to others' needs through prayer.

① **After rereading Nehemiah 1:1-8, answer the following questions.**

Why did Nehemiah pray? List as many reasons as you can find.

_____

_____

_____

What things did Nehemiah mention that showed the intensity or the seriousness of his prayer?

_____

_____

_____

What pattern in Nehemiah's prayer might be useful to others who make intercessory prayer a part of their ministry to others?

_____

_____

_____

Serving others through prayer grows from discovering their needs. Nehemiah was led to intercede in prayer when he discovered the needs of the Jews who had returned from exile (see vv. 2,4). Intercession is more than just asking God to do something for an individual. It connects the intercessor with the individual on a spiritual plane and displays compassion for the person in need. Verse 4 says that Nehemiah "sat down and wept" and "mourned for a number days."

The magnitude of the need and the commitment to pray are displayed in the time the intercessor commits to this act of service. Nehemiah is seen "fasting and praying before the God of heaven" (v. 4). Nehemiah's prayer life also demonstrates the kind of relationship that is needed between the intercessor and God. In verse 6 he prayed, "Let Your eyes be open and Your ears be attentive to hear." Intercessors can also pray confidently when they base their requests on the promises of God. Nehemiah asked God to remember the promise He had given Moses (see v. 8).

2. **Today's practical experience will require you to listen to what people are praying. Choose from these suggestions.**
   • Contact several people in your church who pray for others. Ask them how they intercede.
   • Interview a Bible study leader, a close friend, or a pastor in your church on the topic of interceding in prayer for the needs of others.

3. **After completing your assignment, write in "My Observation Journal" what you are hearing, how it makes you feel, and what you can do to minister to others through prayer.**

4. **Turn to "My Ministry List" on page 92 and write the names of people in your life who have ministry needs.**

5. **Look for an opportunity to tell someone how your memory verse, 1 Peter 4:10, is impacting your view of people and things.**

and ordinances You gave Your servant Moses. [8]Please remember what You commanded Your servant Moses: "If you are unfaithful, I will scatter you among the peoples." ' "
Nehemiah 1:1-8

Serving others through prayer grows from discovering their needs.

My Observation Journal

Watch and Pray
Begin praying regularly for the persons on your ministry list who have ministry needs.

Day 4 • Watch an Encourager

God's Word for Today

"I was a stranger and you took Me in." Matthew 25:35

Read and meditate on "God's Word for Today" in the margin and spend a moment in prayer as you begin today's study.

A teenage girl came to a pregnancy resource center to learn whether she was pregnant. She was in trouble with the law, had been kicked out of school, had been a runaway, and had a history of drug abuse The pregnancy test was positive. After volunteers worked closely with this young woman, she chose to keep the baby and try to turn her life around. She connected with a local church, got back in school, received coaching with homework assignments, attended Bible study sessions with a mentor from the resource center, and received prenatal care. Her life indeed turned around over time, and it started when Christians showed hospitality to her.

It is difficult to influence people for Christ if you don't have relationships with them. Every witnessing relationship begins with investing time and energy in people you don't know. Titus 1:7-9 says that overseers (preachers or ministers) are on the front line in offering hospitality*. What is hospitality? The Greek word for *hospitable* is derived from two words—*philos* (Greek), which refers to showing mutual love to one another, as in the case of brothers, and *xenos* (Greek), meaning *stranger*.

Titus 1:7-9

"An overseer, as God's manager, must be blameless, not arrogant, not quick tempered, not addicted to wine, not a bully, not greedy for money, but hospitable, loving what is good, sensible, righteous, holy, self-controlled, holding to the faithful message as taught, so that he will be able both to encourage with sound teaching and to refute those who contradict it."

1) **How would you define *stranger*?** _____

_____

_____

A stranger is someone outside your neighborhood—someone who is different from you, doesn't know anybody, or is just passing through. If your job takes you out of town, you know the feeling of being away from home, family, and friends. You are lonely, you may be a little anxious, and you probably have excess time on your hands. Basically, a stranger is someone you do not currently know. The Bible teaches us to offer hospitality to strangers.

* *Hospitality:* showing love to a stranger

2) **What are some ways to show hospitality to strangers?** _____

_____

_____

The Old Testament law admonished the Hebrews to receive strangers into their homes and to provide food and shelter. It even commanded them to love strangers as themselves and to care for them (see Leviticus 19:33-34; Deuteronomy 24:17-22). Hospitality also formed a backdrop for Jewish life in the New Testament (see Luke 7:36). In Matthew 25:31-46 Jesus characterized the righteous as those who care for strangers and others in need. The early church taught Christians to show hospitality as an expression of brotherly love (see Hebrews 13:1-2; 1 Peter 4:8-9).

One challenge we face today is overcoming obstacles to hospitality so that we can gain opportunities to serve others and share Christ.

(3) **What obstacles discourage you from showing hospitality?**
○ Time ○ Culture ○ Timidity ○ Insecurity ○ Busyness
○ Motivation ○ Other: _____

Hindrances to hospitality may include any of these factors. It's hard to get excited about connecting with people who are not a part of our circle of family, friends, and acquaintances. Yet establishing a relationship with someone is a critical prerequisite to showing the love of Christ.

(4) **Today observe people who display an awareness of and a response to strangers—people who are not from their neighborhood. Choose one of the following.**
- Ask your pastor for the names of people in your church who contact visitors to the church or newcomers to the community. Ask these people what they do to minister.
- Visit a ministry your church performs or another ministry in your community. Observe the way volunteers engage with individuals who receive ministry.
- Call your local police department, hospital, or military base to learn whether they have a chaplain on duty you can interview. Ask questions about how he connects with strangers.

(5) **Write your observations in "My Observation Journal" in the margin. Describe what you saw, what you learned, how it made you feel, and what you want to do in response.**

(6) **Quote 1 Peter 4:10 and then write it in the margin from memory.**

Leviticus 19:33-34
"When a foreigner lives with you in your land, you must not oppress him. You must regard the foreigner who lives with you as the native-born among you. You are to love him as yourself, for you were foreigners in the land of Egypt; I am the LORD your God."

Hebrews 13:1-2
"Let brotherly love continue. Don't neglect to show hospitality, for by doing this some have welcomed angels as guests without knowing it."

My Observation Journal

Day 5 • Watch a Personal Trainer

God's Word for Today

"⁹For this reason also, since the day we heard this, we haven't stopped praying for you. We are asking that you may be filled with the knowledge of His will in all wisdom and spiritual understanding, ¹⁰so that you may walk worthy of the Lord, fully pleasing to Him, bearing fruit in every good work and growing in the knowledge of God. ¹¹May you be strengthened with all power, according to His glorious might, for all endurance and patience, with joy ¹²giving thanks to the Father, who has enabled you to share in the saints' inheritance in the light. ¹³He has rescued us from the domain of darkness and transferred us into the kingdom of the Son He loves, ¹⁴in whom we have redemption, the forgiveness of sins."
Colossians 1:9-14

↕ Read and meditate on "God's Word for Today" in the margin and spend a moment in prayer as you begin today's study.

Everything that has life grows until it starts to die. Growth is programmed into the human body. Bones grow, teeth come out and are replaced, and metabolism changes to reflect age. Other types of growth are not automatic: muscle development requires exercise; wisdom requires education; and relationships demand time, integrity, and attention.

In a similar way, spiritual growth is not preprogrammed. It is not automatic. It requires development and discipline. Because we are relational beings, nothing is more important in the Christian life than someone you trust to speak words of accountability to you. The words of the Lord Jesus Christ and the letters written by the apostle Paul are filled with specific instructions that lead to spiritual growth. Whether it is to follow through, endure, stay the course, obey, or face great difficulty, the goal of spiritual maturity is always at the forefront of Paul's teachings.

① **Why do you think spiritual growth is important for someone who wants to minister to others?**

_____

The approach taken by two women who came to my (Richard's) door reminded me that knowing what the Bible says is not the sole sign of maturity. They knew what they claimed to be another translation of the Bible. They were schooled in offering rebuttals to my statements. They even used the same terms I used. The problem is, they didn't believe Jesus is fully God. Spiritual maturity is more than acquiring information. It is becoming obedient. We can't effectively attract people to Jesus if we don't grow in His likeness and embody His presence in the world.

Paul's letter to the church at Colossae teaches us several things about the spiritual-growth process. Refer to "God's Word for Today" in the margin as you read the following summary.

1. Paul considered prayer to be an important component of spiritual growth (see v. 9). God always initiates prayer for the things He wants to do.

(2) **What is the general subject of Paul's prayer?** _____

_____

Proverbs 27:17
"Iron sharpens iron, and one man sharpens another."

2. Spiritual growth directly reflects on the Lord. Your growth or lack of growth says something about the Lord Jesus Christ, the One who put you in the position to grow spiritually and the One who enables your growth (see v. 10).

3. Your ability to have an impact in Christ's kingdom hinges on your spiritual growth. When you face difficulty, you will be called to an endurance that is found solely in the strength developed through spiritual growth (see v. 11).

4. God uses multiple means to communicate the steps He wants Christians to take. The Holy Spirit is always at work to convince you (see v. 9). God may also use other believers to speak to you as they respond to God's urging and enabling for their own service in the kingdom (see Prov. 27:17).

Your ability to have an impact in Christ's kingdom hinges on your spiritual growth.

My Observation Journal

(3) **What is the status of your spiritual growth?**
○ Thriving   ○ Surviving   ○ Reviving   ○ Diving

Explain why you answered the way you did.

_____

_____

(4) **Today observe people who display an awareness of and a response to opportunities to grow in Christ. Choose one of the following.**
- Call, e-mail, or visit your Bible study leader or discipleship leader and ask what he or she senses is a need in your personal spiritual growth.
- Ask a family member or friend to appraise your walk with the Lord.
- Ask the Lord to bring you into contact with someone who will tell you about a change God is asking them to make or a step of faith He is asking them to take to conform to His will for their life.

(5) **Record your observations in "My Observation Journal" in the margin. Describe what you saw, what you learned, how it made you feel, and what you want to do in response.**

(6) **Turn to page 93 and complete "Profile of a Servant Lifestyle" for one of the persons you observed ministering this week. Then complete the profile for yourself.**

Watch and Pray
Pray about your response to activity 3. Ask God to show you what He wants you to do to grow in an obedient relationship with Him. Ask Him to enable you to move out in His power to minister to others.

Session 1 • Connecting with God's Activity Around You

Opening Prayer

Establishing Ground Rules
- While you are in the group session, give the group meeting priority.
- Everyone participates in the discussion, and no one dominates.
- Everyone has the right to his own opinion, and all questions are encouraged and respected.
- Anything said in the meeting room is never repeated outside.
- Group members keep prayer lists for ministry needs (p. 92).

Learning Goal
By observing ministry roles in Scripture and through personal observation, you will identify ministry actions that will connect you with God's activity around you.

Reviewing Week 1
1. In pairs or triads take turns reciting your Scripture-memory verse, 1 Peter 4:10. Discuss what this verse teaches about a servant lifestyle.
2. Identify the five ministry actions presented this week (bridge builder, reliever, intercessor, encourager, personal trainer). Define each one.
3. Identify the ministry action illustrated in each of the following Scriptures passages and answer the questions about each passage.
   - Read 2 Corinthian 5:17-21. What is the ministry of reconciliation? What is the message of reconciliation? Who is responsible for the ministry of reconciliation? What does it mean to be an ambassador for Christ?
   - Read Luke 7:11-17. What was Jesus' motivation in providing relief for the grieving mother? Who in your community needs relief from suffering?
   - Read Nehemiah 1:1-8. What was the source of Nehemiah's mourning? What elements in his prayer are important for modern-day intercessors to use?
   - Read Matthew 25:35. How do you define *stranger?* What is hospitality? How much importance does the Bible place on hospitality? Why is hospitality an important practice for someone who ministers to others?

• Read Colossians 1:9-14. Why is the filling of the Holy Spirit critical to spiritual growth? Why is spiritual growth critical to ministry? What are you doing to grow in Christ?

4. Discuss your experiences observing practitioners of the ministry actions you examined this week. Describe the ministries of the persons you observed. How do they illustrate the biblical principles you have studied? How do they embody the qualities listed in "Profile of a Servant Lifestyle" on page 93? Share your observations from each day's "My Observation Journal."

5. What challenges and blessings did you observe? What did you learn? What approaches can you use or adapt?

6. Brainstorm ways believers can practice the ministry actions you studied this week to meet needs and to show the love of Christ in your community.

Ministering to Others

Turn to "My Ministry List" on page 92 and share the names of persons in your life who have ministry and/or salvation needs. You will update this list throughout the study. What have you already done to address these persons' needs or to show God's love to them? What will you commit to do this week?

Praying Together

Pray in pairs about the following.

• Pray for the concerns on your ministry lists and for your role in meeting these needs. Pray for the salvation of anyone on your lists who is lost.

• Share your assessment of whether you demonstrate the qualities in "Profile of a Servant Lifestyle" on page 93. Pray about any areas in which you need to improve.

• Ask God to help you practice the ministry actions you studied this week in order to meet needs and share Christ.

Previewing Week 2

Turn to page 23 and preview the study for the coming week.

Week 2

Confronting Barriers
That Hinder Servanthood

"Even the Son of Man did not come
to be served, but to serve, and to give
His life—a ransom for many."

Mark 10:45

Confronting Barriers That Hinder Servanthood

The world's goal is to wrap itself around us so that we look and act like the culture. It's time for us to be honest about what the world is doing to us. An honest evaluation can be both difficult and damaging to our pride. We would like to ignore the fact that there is a great difference between doing acts of servanthood and actually becoming a servant. Anyone can perform an act of service. However, to initiate behavioral changes that lead to a lifestyle of serving others, our hearts must be transformed. Unfortunately, because human beings are basically selfish creatures, we must be willing to admit and confront the ungodly barriers that hinder us from becoming the servants Christ desires us to be.

LEARNING GOAL

This week you will—
• examine Scriptures that address surrendering to a lifestyle of servanthood;
• identify barriers to servanthood;
• recognize behaviors that require personal change;
• learn simple ways to serve others;
• understand the imperative of servanthood in Christlike ministry to others.

OVERVIEW OF WEEK 2

Day 1: The Barrier of Materialism
Day 2: The Barrier of Entitlement
Day 3: The Barrier of Pride
Day 4: The Barrier of Spiritual Blindness
Day 5: The Barrier of Unconfessed Sin

VERSE TO MEMORIZE

Mark 10:45

DISCIPLESHIP HELPS FOR WEEK 2

My Ministry List (p. 92)
Ideas for Ministry Actions (pp. 94–98)

Day 1 • The Barrier of Materialism

God's Word for Today

"Looking at him, Jesus loved him and said to him, 'You lack one thing: Go, sell all you have and give to the poor, and you will have treasure in heaven. Then come, follow Me.'"
Mark 10:21

Read and meditate on "God's Word for Today" in the margin and spend a moment in prayer as you begin today's lesson.

The rich young man, whose story is told in Mark 10:17-22, is not much different from many people today. Though obviously a very religious and pious man, he still lacked what Christ desires most from His children: he was unwilling to give up everything for the sake of following the Savior. Unfortunately, his attachment to this world prevented him from inheriting eternal life.

People don't have to be wealthy to be attached to the world. Many who are not wealthy nonetheless have materialistic values, believing material goods will bring happiness and self-fulfillment. Prisons are filled with people willing to risk their lives and integrity for the sake of materialism. We live in a consumer culture. Men and women today spend more time at work than at any time in history to finance their enormous appetite for more. Could it be that we are so addicted to material things and the high of buying that we have become like drug addicts looking for their next fix? Even Christians are willing to sacrifice the quality of their fellowship with Christ in order to obtain more things.

Even Christians are willing to sacrifice the quality of their fellowship with Christ in order to obtain more things.

1. **How would you complete the following statement? Be brutally honest! I consider myself to be—**
   ○ unimpressed with material things;
   ○ moderately impressed with material things;
   ○ totally consumed with material things.

   In which category would you place the rich young man?

   _____

   What evidence does Mark 10 provide to support your answer?

   _____

   _____

Most likely, you fall into the middle category. As I (David) see it, this is where the rich young man was. He could have gone either way. After all, he knew the commandments and seemed to be fairly committed to God, even as a youth (see Mark 10:20). The problem is, although he was a good person, the rich young man wouldn't let go of his wealth to follow Christ.

How about you? Take a minute to pray about your attitude toward material things. Then check the statement that best describes you.
○ I am willing to give up everything for the sake of the gospel.
○ I prefer a moderate faith.

2 **Carefully read Matthew 6:19-24. Honestly rank the following priorities in your life by numbering them 1 to 8, with 1 being the highest.**
___ Family ___ Relationship with Christ
___ Job advancement ___ Personal integrity
___ Recreation/hobbies ___ Serving others
___ Obtaining nicer things ___ Education

It isn't wrong to want a better life for you and your family. However, it is imperative not to be a slave of money (see v. 24). You can't attract other people to Christ if your ultimate loyalty lies somewhere else. Furthermore, genuine ministry in Christ's name requires a lifestyle of giving instead of getting. Jesus addressed the rich young man in Mark 10:21 because He loved him. Jesus knew that life is never about what we receive; it is the selfless acts of giving and following Him that matter.

3 **Jesus instructed the rich young man to "sell all you have and give to the poor, and you will have treasure in heaven. Then come, follow Me." Serving others, including the poor, is one way to follow Christ. Think of ways you can begin serving others today.**
• If it is raining, use your umbrella to escort someone into the grocery store or shopping center.
• Be kind at your place of employment, a local restaurant, or a shopping center by donating five minutes to open the door for others. Tell them that God loves them or just smile and see how people respond.

For more ideas review "Ideas for Ministry Actions" on pages 94–98. Update "My Ministry List" on page 92 as needed.

4 **Start memorizing your memory verse for this week, Mark 10:45. If you would like, tear out and use the card at the back of the book.**

Matthew 6:19-24
"Don't collect for yourselves treasures on earth, where moth and rust destroy and where thieves break in and steal. But collect for yourselves treasures in heaven, where neither moth nor rust destroys, and where thieves don't break in and steal. For where your treasure is, there your heart will be also. ... No one can be a slave of two masters, since either he will hate one and love the other, or be devoted to one and despise the other. You cannot be slaves of God and of money."

Watch and Pray
Ask God to free you from the bondage of materialism and to help you set your priorities around His desires, not the world's.

Day 2 • The Barrier of Entitlement

God's Word for Today

"James and John, the sons of Zebedee, approached Him and said, 'Teacher, we want You to do something for us if we ask You?' 'What do you want Me to do for you?' He asked them. They answered Him, 'Allow us to sit at Your right and Your left in Your glory.' But Jesus said to them, 'You don't know what you're asking. Are you able to drink the cup I drink or to be baptized with the baptism I am baptized with?' 'We are able,' they told Him."
Mark 10:35–39

✱ *Entitlement:* The idea that someone deserves preferential treatment. It is the opposite of being a servant, who is willing to give up one's life to follow Christ, regardless of the cost.

Read and meditate on "God's Word for Today" in the margin and spend a moment in prayer as you begin today's lesson.

My (David's) mother tells the story of visiting a church one Sunday after the death of my father. She arrived early enough to seat herself in an almost empty sanctuary. Grieving and lonely, she was encouraged when an older woman approached her and began to speak. However, her warm feelings soon dissipated when the woman ignored my mother's greeting and quickly reminded her that as a member of the church since its inception 45 years ago, she had always sat in the seat my mother had chosen. Without compassion she forced this grieving widow to slide over if she wanted to sit in her area of the sanctuary.

Unfortunately, incidents like this are common occurrences in congregations where an entitlement* mentality is allowed to exist without being challenged. The opposite of being a servant, it is the same attitude James and John displayed in Mark 10:35-39—me first, others later!

1. **Are you suffering from the same spirit of entitlement as James and John? Beside each statement write *T* for *true* or *F* for *false*.**
   ___ I often complain about church decisions, being concerned only with my desires, regardless of how they affect the unsaved.
   ___ I believe I deserve to be treated better at church because I am a longtime member.
   ___ I believe the church staff should cater to my needs first before ministering to the unsaved.
   ___ I am threatened by change and especially by newcomers to church.

Are you any different from James and John or the woman my mother met at church? Pray and ask God to reveal any areas of entitlement in your life. Record those areas below.

_____

To fully understand how inconsiderate a spirit of entitlement can be, notice the startling announcement Jesus made just moments before being approached by James and John.

② **Read Mark 10:33-34 in the margin. How does Jesus' example compare to James and John's request?**

_____

_____

After hearing Jesus' prediction, how could anyone be concerned about themselves? What about Jesus' well-being? What about His example of surrender to the Father's will? No one in history deserved more honor and glory; yet He surrendered it all to make salvation possible.

③ **Read Jesus' words in Matthew 16:24-25. What is the solution to an attitude of entitlement?**

_____

_____

Jesus said, "Whoever loses his life because of Me will find it." The only way to lose your life is to give it away and live for others, regardless of the way they treat you in return. That's the attitude of a servant of Christ.

④ **Identify a time in the past six months when you surrendered yourself to serve someone else, not expecting anything in return.**

_____

_____

_____

⑤ **If you haven't served someone this way, why?**
○ Entitlement   ○ Other priorities   ○ Haven't embraced servanthood
○ Other: _____

⑥ **Complete the following sentences.**
• To deny myself, I must give up _____.
• To take up my cross, I must be willing to _____.
• To follow Christ, I must learn to _____.

⑦ **Write this week's memory verse.** _____

_____

_____

Mark 10:33-34

"Listen! We are going to Jerusalem. The Son of Man will be handed over to the chief priests and the scribes, and they will condemn Him to death. Then they will hand Him over to the Gentiles, and they will mock Him, spit on Him, flog Him, and kill Him, and He will rise after three days."

Matthew 16:24-25

"If anyone wants to come with Me, he must deny himself, take up his cross, and follow Me. For whoever wants to save his life will lose it, but whoever loses his life because of Me will find it."

↕ **Watch and Pray**

Pray about your attitude toward God. Do you treat Him as though He owes you more than He has already given you? Confess any sense of entitlement and ask God to develop in you a heart of servanthood that wants to minister in His name.

Day 3 • The Barrier of Pride

"Jesus called them over and said to them, 'You know that those who are regarded as rulers of the Gentiles dominate them, and their men of high positions exercise power over them. But it must not be like that among you. On the contrary, whoever wants to become great among you must be your servant, and whoever wants to be first among you must be a slave to all. For even the Son of Man did not come to be served, but to serve, and to give His life—a ransom for many.'"
Mark 10:42-45

Read and meditate on "God's Word for Today" in the margin and spend a moment in prayer as you begin today's lesson.

From yesterday's study you already know the background of "God's Word for Today"—James and John's selfish request to sit at Jesus' right and left in glory. At the heart of the issue is sinful pride and a misunderstanding of the way Christ defines real influence and power.

1. How does the world define influence and power? Check the words that apply or add some of your own.
   - ○ Money
   - ○ Serving others
   - ○ Position in society
   - ○ Humility
   - ○ Being the boss
   - ○ Selflessness
   - _____
   - _____
   - _____

2. How did Jesus define influence and power in Mark 10:42-45? Circle some of the defining words in the Scripture in the margin.

Pride will never result in a servant spirit that sees others as more important than personal needs. Jesus said if someone wants to achieve greatness, he must be willing to become a servant; and if he wants to be first, he must be "a slave to all" (v. 44).

3. What does it mean to be a servant and a slave? _____
   _____

4. Write this week's memory verse, Mark 10:45, in the margin. Why did Jesus come?
   _____

Jesus gave His life to humble service, and He taught His followers to do the same.

Proverbs 16:18
"Pride comes before destruction, and an arrogant spirit before a fall."

Read Proverbs 16:18 in the margin. Is pride destroying your witness? Stop and ask God to reveal any areas of destructive pride in your life that are hindering a selfless life of Christlike surrender. Be transparent. Confess your pride and ask for forgiveness.

The primary quality of a servant is humility. In Luke 18:9-14 Jesus told a parable to illustrate the value of humility in His kingdom. In verse 14 He concluded, "Everyone who exalts himself will be humbled, but the one who humbles himself will be exalted." God exalts a person only when he does not take credit for his service and willingly surrenders all the glory to Him.

⑤ **Read Luke 18:9-14 in your Bible and answer the following questions.**

Which man was more representative of the humble servant spirit that Christ desires from His children? ○ Pharisee ○ Tax collector

Which man are you most like in your spiritual life?
○ Pharisee ○ Tax collector

⑥ **Name two persons you know who exemplify genuine humility.**

_____

What qualities make these persons servants? _____

_____

_____

The opposite of selfish pride is to become a selfless servant of God and others. Jesus gave us a model for servanthood when He washed the disciples' feet (see John 13:1-5). Washing feet was the most humiliating act a person could perform in Jewish society; yet Jesus willingly took up the towel and became a slave, even to the point of dying on the cross.

⑦ **Today humbly wash the feet of someone you know—your spouse, a friend, or a family member. Don't be shy; it is a powerful testimony to the humility and love of Christ. Then record your feelings and impressions in "My Observation Journal" in the margin.**

⑧ **Identify two things you can do to demonstrate a servant spirit to someone who needs to see the love of Christ.**

_____

_____

When you minister to someone, remember to update "My Ministry List" on page 92.

> The opposite of selfish pride is to become a selfless servant of God and others.

> **My Observation Journal**

> ↕ **Watch and Pray**
> Spend time in prayer. Humble yourself before God and exalt Him as your Lord. Pray for a spirit of humility in serving others that exemplifies the character and love of Christ.

Day 4 • The Barrier of Spiritual Blindness

God's Word for Today

"As He was leaving Jericho with His disciples and a large crowd, Bartimaeus (the son of Timaeus), a blind beggar, was sitting by the road. When he heard that it was Jesus the Nazarene, he began to cry out, 'Son of David, Jesus, have mercy on me!' Many people told him to keep quiet, but he was crying out all the more, 'Have mercy on me, Son of David!' Jesus stopped and said, 'Call him.' So they called the blind man and said to him, 'Have courage! Get up; He's calling for you.' He threw off his coat, jumped up, and came to Jesus. Then Jesus answered him, 'What do you want Me to do for you?' 'Rabbouni,' the blind man told Him, 'I want to see!' 'Go your way,' Jesus told him. 'Your faith has healed you.' Immediately he could see and began to follow Him on the road." Mark 10:46-52

Read and meditate on "God's Word for Today" in the margin and spend a moment in prayer as you begin today's lesson.

I (David) once approached a seminary professor during an exam and inquired about a true/false question that used the word *always* in reference to the way scholars interpret a certain passage of Scripture. I will never forget my professor's response: "If you said a cloudless sky is always blue, someone would find a reason to disagree, especially in Baptist circles." I smiled, returned to my seat, and decided the question was probably false.

Unfortunately, my professor's assertion was correct in more areas than biblical interpretation. As a young pastor, I was quickly initiated to the reality of negative people with extreme spiritual blindness. Like the negative people who attacked Bartimaeus when he was begging for mercy, many others in the church today are indifferent to spiritual issues. Consider the following questions.

- How can Christians pass by people like Bartimaeus without hurting for their plight in life? Is there ever a good excuse not to care?
- If not, how do we treat people like Bartimaeus? Is our first response to judge the person without caring for their needs? When we see a homeless person, do we say, "They need to get a job" or "If they weren't so lazy, they could make it"? Do we automatically assume the worst without considering the vast opportunities for ministry?
- Has the church become a crowd of overly religious people ignoring the plight of a hurting world and conveniently telling everyone to be quiet? Is the church spiritually blind?
- To the credit of Bartimaeus, he continued to summon Jesus, and a miracle followed as he receive his sight. Is it possible that Christians have become so blind, negative, and self-absorbed that we are missing the daily miracles of Christ?

In an attitude of prayer, read the previous questions and ask God to reveal any spiritual blindness you may have. Ask Him to remove the blinders so that you can see Him at work, recognize needs around you, and genuinely care about and minister to others.

A key area of spiritual blindness for many Christians is prejudice*—an unholy attitude toward people of other races, cultures, and economic status.

1. **Read the following passages in your Bible and record the type of prejudice or the unholy attitude illustrated.**
   Mark 10:13-16: _____
   John 8:1-11: _____
   Matthew 9:1-8: _____
   Matthew 9:10-13: _____

   Now read Matthew 7:1-5 in the margin. How does Jesus' teaching apply to our attitudes and actions toward people of different backgrounds and races?

   _____
   _____
   _____

Another common form of spiritual blindness is disobedience. In Matthew 25:14-30 Jesus told a parable about people who say no to God's work in their lives instead of allowing Him to multiply their talents.

2. **Read Matthew 25:14-30 in your Bible. Are you willing to humble yourself and serve the unsaved, regardless of how difficult and inconvenient it may be, or are you saying no to God?**

   _____

3. **Review "Ideas for Ministry Actions" on pages 94–98. List three immediate actions you can take to serve outside your comfort zone. An example is volunteering at a homeless shelter or at a pregnancy resource center.**
   1. _____
   2. _____
   3. _____

   Update "My Ministry List" on page 92 as you minister to others.

It is time for Christians to stop creating roadblocks to ministry. Instead of acting like Pharisees, we must take off the blinders and learn to love people unconditionally. Only then can we truly minister in Jesus' name.

Matthew 7:1-5
"Do not judge, so that you won't be judged. For with the judgment you use, you will be judged, and with the measure you use, it will be measured to you. Why do you look at the speck in your brother's eye but don't notice the log in your own eye? Or how can you say to your brother, 'Let me take the speck out of your eye,' and look, there's a log in your eye? Hypocrite! First take the log out of your eye, and then you will see clearly to take the speck out of your brother's eye."

✳ Prejudice: preconceived judgment or hostility without just grounds or adequate knowledge

Watch and Pray
Pray for God to clear your heart of any prejudice that would hinder your service.

Day 5 • The Barrier of Unconfessed Sin

God's Word for Today

"Be gracious to me, God, according to Your faithful love; according to Your abundant compassion, blot out my rebellion. Wash away my guilt, and cleanse me from my sin. For I am conscious of my rebellion, and my sin is always before me. Against You—You alone—I have sinned and done this evil in Your sight. So You are right when You pass sentence; You are blameless when You judge. Indeed, I was guilty when I was born; I was sinful when my mother conceived me."
Psalm 51:1-5

Read and meditate on "God's Word for Today" in the margin and spend a moment in prayer as you begin today's lesson.

In his book *Beneath the Surface* Bob Reccord shares a story about confronting a close friend who was involved in an ongoing affair. As a result, the man's wife left him, and he lost his job as a minister.

Reccord asked the man, "How could you do it? Didn't you realize what was happening? Weren't there alarms going off, at least when the affair was in danger of beginning?" After an extended time of silence, the man responded, "Yes, Bob. There were warnings. I heard the alarms of my conscience and God's Word clanging in my life … but I decided to disconnect the wires."[1]

Unfortunately, this response is exactly what David described in Psalm 51. The background of the passage is found in 2 Samuel 12:1-15, when Nathan the prophet rebuked King David for disconnecting his spiritual wires after committing adultery with Bathsheba. David went even further by trying to cover his sin; as a result, Bathsheba's husband, Uriah, was killed. In the end David lost the respect of much of Israel and almost lost his kingdom to Absalom.

1. Review Psalm 51:1-5 in the margin. Underline any words or phrases that refer to David's confession of his personal sin.

   List words or phrases David used to identify the attributes of God to which he appealed as He sought forgiveness.

   _____

   _____

Romans 3:23
"All have sinned and fall short of the glory of God."

2. Read Romans 3:23 in the margin. Since "all have sinned," what words or phrases would you use in reference to your sin if you were writing Psalm 51?

   _____

   _____

In reference to "the glory of God," list words you would use to describe God's forgiveness.

_____

_____

The essence of sin* is total selfishness and a desire to be like God and to know what He knows. Infatuation with self becomes a stumbling block to Christ's call for His followers to become servants and slaves to the world (see Mark 10:42-45). If left unconfessed, this sin of self-exaltation will overtake a Christian's life and make our hearts calloused to the needs of others. It is impossible to be a true servant and self-absorbed at the same time. As John the Baptist stated in John 3:30, "He [Jesus] must increase, but I must decrease."

 Sin: a spiritual state of rebellion against God that causes people to break His laws and fall short of His intentions for their lives

③ **Search your heart and complete the following statements in regard to your personal sins.**

I wrestle with God over …

_____

_____

I would become a better servant and slave to others if I …

_____

_____

Infatuation with self becomes a stumbling block to Christ's call for His followers to become servants and slaves to the world.

④ **What changes are needed in your life for you to decrease and for Jesus to increase?**

_____

_____

⑤ **Carefully read David's response to God's forgiveness in Psalm 51:6-17, paying special attention to the descriptive terms he used.**

⑥ **Respond to God's forgiveness soon by ministering to a stranger. Record the results in "My Ministry List" on page 92.**

⑦ **Write this week's memory verse.** _____

_____

_____

Watch and Pray
Spend time in prayer confessing any sin that is hindering your becoming the surrendered servant God wants you to be. Reread Psalm 51:10-13, applying it personally whenever the pronoun *me* is used.

Week 2 » Day 5

1. Bob Reccord, *Beneath the Surface* (Nashville: Broadman & Holman, 2002), 36.

Session 2 • Confronting Barriers That Hinder Servanthood

Opening Prayer

Learning Goal

You will—

- examine Scriptures that address surrendering to a lifestyle of servanthood;
- identify barriers to servanthood;
- recognize behaviors that require personal change;
- learn simple ways to serve others;
- understand the imperative of servanthood in Christlike ministry to others.

Reviewing Week 2

1. In pairs or triads take turns reciting your Scripture-memory verse, Mark 10:45. Discuss Jesus' example of servanthood.

2. Identify the five barriers to servanthood that were presented this week (materialism, entitlement, pride, spiritual blindness, unconfessed sin). Briefly describe how they discourage ministry to others.

3. Christians are not immune to materialism. What are issues that tempt Christians to stray from complete surrender to Christ as servants to Him and others? What is your greatest challenge in this area?

4. It has been said that worldly, materialistic values are hindering the church from being salt and light to the unsaved. Do you think this is true? If so, what are some issues that need to be addressed?

5. What lessons did you learn from Mark 10:35-39? Respond to the true/false activity (activity 1) on page 26.

6. Read Matthew 16:24-25. How does Christ's proclamation differ from the worldly mind-set of entitlement?

7. Read Mark 10:42-45. Discuss what it means to be a servant. How does this concept differ from the attitude of secular society? What does it look like to be a slave? How does this understanding transform the approach you take in your ministry to others?

8. Share experiences washing someone's feet (activity 7, p. 29). What did you learn about Christ through the experience? What did you learn about yourself? If you refused to wash feet, why?

9. Respond to the series of questions on page 30. Why do you think these attitudes exist among believers? How does a negative response to people in need match up with Scripture and Jesus' call to be a servant?

10. In what ways have you been spiritually blind to the needs of people in your sphere of influence? Are you too busy? Or like the Pharisees, are you blinded by the walls of religion?

11. Name sins that hinder believers from becoming the servants God desires.

12. Are there other barriers to becoming a servant that were not covered this week?

13. Based on Scripture and what you have learned this week, discuss how your church could immediately start reflecting the biblical model of service by ministering to the surrounding community.

Ministering to Others

1. Share ideas for practicing servanthood as a daily lifestyle. Start with these suggestions. Also see "Ideas for Ministry Actions" on pages 94–98.
   - Begin in your home by assisting with chores before being reminded. This is especially effective in reaching teenagers and unsaved spouses and family members.
   - Purchase a cup of coffee for someone while in line at a coffee shop or purchase a meal for an individual or a family at a restaurant. If they ask why, share a brief testimony about God's grace.
   - Practice servanthood by slowing down and seeing needs, opening doors, listening to others, actively caring, and so on.

2. Examine "My Ministry List" on page 92. What have you done this week to address these persons' needs or to show God's love to them? What will you commit to do this week? Who needs to be added?

Praying Together

Share changes you will immediately make to become a servant who ministers in Jesus' name. Pray for these commitments in groups of three or four. Also pray that God will help you overcome barriers to a lifestyle of servanthood. Finally, pray for the persons on your ministry lists.

Previewing Week 2

Turn to page 37 and preview the study for the coming week.

Week 3

Assessing Ministry Needs,
Impacting Hurting People

"Don't you say, 'There are still four months,
then comes the harvest'? Listen to what
I'm telling you: Open your eyes and look
at the fields, for they are ready for harvest."

John 4:35

Assessing Ministry Needs, Impacting Hurting People

When we act without looking, we reveal the depth of our selfishness. When we look without seeing, we limit our impact to the extent of our understanding. But when we take the time to ask questions, we create relationships that ultimately change lives. To become servants, Christians must first learn to assess the needs of those who are hurting. All too often, the church appears to turn a deaf ear to those needing assistance. Is it because the church doesn't care, or have Christians simply forgotten how to acknowledge the needs of others? Is the church blind or just complacent? In either case, assessing needs is imperative to the ultimate goal of meeting needs, thus awakening the church to its call to minister to a desperately hurting world.

LEARNING GOAL
This week you will—
• identify places where needs exist;
• learn what the Bible says about assessing and meeting needs;
• discover ways Jesus responded to people in need;
• identify simple ways to meet needs;
• adopt a lifestyle of meeting needs on a daily basis.

OVERVIEW OF WEEK 3
Day 1: Going Where the Needs Are
Day 2: Assessing Needs
Day 3: Developing a Ministry Plan
Day 4: Putting the Plan to Work
Day 5: Completing the Task

VERSE TO MEMORIZE
John 4:35

DISCIPLESHIP HELPS FOR WEEK 3
My Ministry List (p. 92)
Ministry Action Plan (p. 99)
Community Prayerwalking (p. 100)

Day 1 • Going Where the Needs Are

God's Word for Today

"He [Jesus] came to a town of Samaria called Sychar. ... A woman of Samaria came to draw water. 'Give Me a drink,' Jesus said to her, for His disciples had gone into town to buy food. 'How is it that You, a Jew, ask for a drink from me, a Samaritan woman?' she asked Him. For Jews do not associate with Samaritans."
John 4:5-9

Matthew 9:10-13

"While He [Jesus] was reclining at the table in the house, many tax collectors and sinners came as guests to eat with Jesus and His disciples. When the Pharisees saw this, they asked His disciples, 'Why does your Teacher eat with tax collectors and sinners?' But when He heard this, He said, 'Those who are well don't need a doctor, but the sick do. Go and learn what this means: "I desire mercy and not sacrifice." For I didn't come to call the righteous, but sinners.'"

Read and meditate on "God's Word for Today" in the margin and spend a moment in prayer as you begin today's lesson.

There is an old saying, "I don't drink, smoke, or chew or go with girls who do!" Some may find the statement humorous, and it was the first 20 times I (David) heard it. However, it's a different story when we apply the spirit of this statement to our ministry to needy people.

Of course, I'm not referring to dating or girls, especially since I've been married for 25 years! The point is, when we are unwilling to associate with certain types of people because we consider them desperate sinners or because our hearts are filled with prejudice, we are disobeying God's call to show the love of Jesus to them.

Jesus demonstrated the right attitude in John 4. It was unheard of for a Jewish male to knowingly associate with a Samaritan, especially a Samaritan woman in public. After all, Jews hated Samaritans with a passion. This woman, an adulterer, would have been despised most of all. The vast majority of Jews would have never risked going through Samaria in the first place, but John 4:4 says that Jesus "had to travel through Samaria." To the average Jew, this woman had no hope of spiritual redemption. However, Jesus was not the average Jew.

1. **Who initiated the conversation in John 4:5-9?**
   ○ The Samaritan woman   ○ Jesus

This woman had a spiritual need. Jesus was willing to go where He knew the need existed and to take the initiative to meet the need, even though it meant breaking out of social norms and associating with an outcast.

2. **Read Matthew 9:10-13 in the margin and answer the questions.**

   When Jesus said He came for those who are sick, what need was He addressing?
   ○ Mental illness   ○ Sin   ○ Social ills   ○ Physical sickness

What do you think Jesus meant when He told the Pharisees, "I desire mercy and not sacrifice"?

_____

Jesus made it clear that He came to meet the needs of those the Pharisees rejected. He offered mercy for their sins, not ritual, as the way they could be right with God.

Jesus made it clear that He came to meet the needs of those the Pharisees rejected.

3 How do Jesus' words apply to the way you and your church should approach people in need?

_____

Jesus demonstrated the same willingness to reach out to sinners when He intiated a relationship with Zacchaeus.

4 Read the account of Jesus and Zacchaeus in Luke 19:1-10 from your Bible. Why do you think Jesus wanted to go to the home of a hated tax collector?

_____

In Luke 19:10 Jesus summed up His ministry this way: "The Son of Man has come to seek and to save the lost." Throughout His earthly ministry Jesus was willing to seek and associate with lost people in order to bring them into a relationship with the Father.

Key Places for Ministry
1.
2.
3.
4.
5.

5 Check the statement you most closely agree with.
○ Christians should avoid places where unsaved people hang out and sin is rampant to avoid compromising their witness.
○ Christians must go where lost people are and associate with sinners in order to show them God's love and mercy.

6 List in the margin five key spots in your community where you can find unsaved persons. Pray for these places and persons. Then visit one or more places in the next week to meet lost persons' needs. Clean restrooms, randomly purchase a meal for someone, or ask the manager how you can serve. Update "My Ministry List" (p. 92) as you minister.

7 Start memorizing your memory verse for this week, John 4:35. If you would like, tear out and use the card at the back of the book.

Watch and Pray
Pray for God to give you a heart of love and mercy to look beyond what others may think and go serve hurting and unsaved people.

Day 2 • Assessing Needs

God's Word for Today

"Jesus answered, 'If you knew the gift of God, and who is saying to you, "Give Me a drink," you would have asked Him, and He would have given you living water.' 'Sir,' said the woman, 'You don't even have a bucket, and the well is deep. So where do you get this "living water"?' … Jesus said, 'Everyone who drinks from this water will get thirsty again. But whoever drinks from the water that I will give him will never get thirsty again—ever! In fact, the water I will give him will become a well of water springing up within him for eternal life.' 'Sir,' the woman said to Him, 'give me this water so I won't get thirsty and come here to draw water.'"
John 4:10-15

Read and meditate on "God's Word for Today" in the margin and spend a moment in prayer as you begin today's lesson.

Many Christians live in a safe, if not imaginary, world that is detached from the real needs of hurting people. For example:
• Do we really know our neighbors?
• Do we really know our coworkers?
• Do we really know our families?

By using the word *know*, I (David) am not referring to awareness of people in these relational spheres. It is not enough to simply recognize people's names or faces. Think about it. People might be struggling with critical issues of health, finances, marriage, persistent sin, or spiritual matters. Wouldn't you want to know so that you could help?

Jesus was a master of assessing people's real needs. For instance, notice how He responded to the woman at the well in John 4.

1) **Reread John 4:10-15 in the margin. Check the methods Jesus used to assess the woman's need.**
   ○ Listened   ○ Connected physical need to spiritual need
   ○ Argued   ○ Pointed to the way of salvation

Note the tone of Jesus' responses. He began with the woman's physical need—water—and probed her heart to assess her greatest need—salvation. By first listening to the woman and wisely, sensitively probing, He was able to get her to open up about her life. In contrast, when the disciples returned to the scene, they demonstrated a complete lack of spiritual awareness of the woman's need.

2) **Read John 4:27-35 in your Bible. Contrast the disciples' response to the woman at the well with that of Jesus. Beside each characteristic write *D* to indicate the disciples' response and *J* to indicate Jesus'.**
   ___ Uncaring   ___ Willing to assist   ___ Servant   ___ Loving
   ___ Compassionate   ___ Willing to connect   ___ Cold   ___ Blind
   ___ Disconnected   ___ Distracted   ___ Relational

The disciples in John 4 obviously wanted to get Jesus fed and out of Samaria as soon as possible. In John 4:35 Jesus challenged them to open their eyes to the spiritual needs around them.

3) John 4:35 is this week's memory verse. Write it here.

_____

_____

_____

To assess the needs of others, you first have to be willing to see the needs. This will require time. Slow down and notice the needs around you every day. It takes time to see needs, especially if they are outside your circle of relationships.

4) Briefly describe the last time you responded to the need of a hurting person who was outside your normal sphere of acquaintances. Did you make the connection to their spiritual need? If so, how?

_____

_____

Jesus was the epitome of empathy.

Seeing needs also requires empathy. You have to deeply care for people and to feel their pain, like Jesus at the tomb of Lazarus. John 11:35 says, "Jesus wept." Even though Jesus knew He would raise Lazarus from the dead, He still wept. Why? Because He cared for Lazarus and hurt for Mary and Martha in their grief. Jesus was the epitome of empathy.

Ministry Opportunities

5) How would you characterize your sensitivity to the needs of others?
○ Compassionate ○ Distracted ○ Blind ○ Sensitive to the Spirit

⬍ Take 30 minutes to seriously assess your home, workplace, and neighborhood for ministry opportunities. Make a list in the margin or on a separate sheet of paper to pray over.

6) Meet the need of one stranger today. It can be as small as washing the windshield for someone at a gas station or purchasing a cup of coffee for someone. Prayerfully assess the situation and be open to the leadership of the Holy Spirit. Remember to record your ministry on "My Ministry List," page 92.

⬍ **Watch and Pray**
Pray that God will open your eyes to see and your heart to empathize with hurting and needy people around you.

Day 3 • Developing a Ministry Plan

God's Word for Today

"One of His disciples, Andrew, Simon Peter's brother, said to Him, 'There's a boy here who has five barley loaves and two fish—but what are they for so many?' Then Jesus said, 'Have the people sit down.' There was plenty of grass in that place, so they sat down. The men numbered about 5,000. Then Jesus took the loaves, and after giving thanks He distributed them to those who were seated—so also with the fish, as much as they wanted. When they were full, He told His disciples, 'Collect the leftovers so that nothing is wasted.' So they collected them and filled 12 baskets with the pieces from the barley loaves that were left over by those who had eaten."
John 6:8-13

↕ Read and meditate on "God's Word for Today" in the margin and spend a moment in prayer as you begin today's lesson.

Several years ago I (David) had a neighbor who was approaching retirement, lived alone, and obviously had several health problems. Her actions and attitude made it plain that she didn't want assistance from or fellowship with her neighbors. It was as if she had a large, flashing neon sign with the message "Leave me alone!" Nevertheless, my wife and I could not get her off our hearts. We knew God was at work, no matter how difficult the situation appeared. So we began to develop a ministry plan. The first step was to begin praying for the neighbor and her needs. We specifically prayed for the person, for wisdom, and for opportunities to serve in the name of Christ.

The next step was to look for ministry opportunities by assessing the situation. Because of her obvious health issues, we noticed that yard work and small upkeep jobs on the house were difficult for her to complete.

We then developed a ministry plan. After going out of our way to smile and acknowledge the neighbor for several weeks, I began to mow and trim her yard. My children pulled weeds from her garden, and my wife baked treats. We showered the person with love by smiling, being genuine, and meeting practical needs. In the end this reclusive neighbor responded by asking how she could have the same faith and peace we had.

1. Do you have a neighbor, friend, coworker, or family member who seems closed to Jesus' love? Does the situation seem impossible, like the situation described in John 6? Write the person's name on "My Ministry List," page 92.

↕ Stop and pray for the person in that "impossible" situation.

John 6:8-13 ("God's Word for Today") illustrates the way Christians can learn to see needs, follow God's direction to create a ministry plan, and then trust God to meet the needs through us. John 2:1-12 describes another occasion when Jesus saw a need and executed a plan to meet it.

2. **Reread John 2:1-12 and answer the following questions.**

   a. What was the need? _____

   _____

   b. How did Jesus respond to the need? _____

   _____

   c. How did the disciples respond (v. 11)? _____

   _____

Notice that Jesus was willing to be in a place where He could help others when a need arose. He was out among people who desperately needed to experience His grace and mercy. Also notice the masterful way Jesus quickly devised a plan and responded to meet the immediate need in a way that brought glory to God. Verse 11 says, "He displayed His glory, and His disciples believed in Him."

Here are some practical steps you can take to formulate a ministry plan. You can remember them by the acrostic SERVE.

S *Search* your heart and check your motives through intimate prayer. Nothing significant ever occurs for God without prayer. Ask God to give you sensitivity to the needs of others.

E *Evaluate* the needs around you by opening your heart and your eyes. Slow down and allow yourself to see and experience the needs. Ask God to give you wisdom and a plan to meet the needs.

R *Resource* the need by considering funds, food, equipment, and so on. Be generous and open to ways God may lead you to meet the needs of others. It doesn't require wealth but faithfulness.

V *Vacate* your comfort zone and put your plan into action. Don't just talk about the need. Go meet it!

E *Evaluate* the response to improve future ministry. If something works, how can you improve it? If it fails, ask why; then don't repeat it.

3. **What are one or two immediate needs you could meet for the person you identified on the previous page? Record these needs on "My Ministry List," page 92.**

Use the SERVE approach to create a ministry plan, using "Ministry Action Plan" on page 99. Then follow your plan to meet a need this week. Record the person's response in "My Observation Journal" in the margin.

Jesus quickly devised a plan and responded to meet the immediate need in a way that brought glory to God.

My Observation Journal

Watch and Pray
Pray that God will give you the best approach to reach the hurts and needs of persons in your sphere of relationships.

Day 4 • Putting the Plan to Work

God's Word for Today

" 'You will receive power when the Holy Spirit has come upon you, and you will be My witnesses in Jerusalem, in all Judea and Samaria, and to the ends of the earth.' After He had said this, He was taken up as they were watching, and a cloud received Him out of their sight. While He was going, they were gazing into heaven, and suddenly two men in white clothes stood by them. They said, 'Men of Galilee, why do you stand looking up into heaven? This Jesus, who has been taken from you into heaven, will come in the same way that you have seen Him going into heaven.' " Acts 1:8-11

Read and meditate on "God's Word for Today" in the margin and spend a moment in prayer as you begin today's lesson.

Several years ago I (David) spoke at a church about its need to immediately sow its community with intentional acts of kindness in order to create gospel conversations. The pastor, though evangelistic, didn't think his people would respond positively to such an approach. He was surprised when over three-fourths of his congregation responded to the simple invitation to serve others in the name of Christ. Unfortunately, he did not feel the same excitement.

I talked with the pastor several months later. When I asked him how the servant activities were going, his response surprised me. He said, "We haven't done anything yet because we are waiting for our matching vests to arrive." It seems that he thought the church should approach the community with similar attire, so he had ordered matching church vests. By the time the vests came in several months later, the congregation had lost its initial zeal for lack of immediate follow-up.

Too often we are more concerned about "vests" than about our communities. We don't need vests. The essential steps are to pray, see the need, establish a plan, and go meet the need. Everything else is irrevelant.

According to Acts 1:8, ministry needs to begin in Jerusalem (our immediate neighborhood, home, work, school); progress to Judea (the larger community, workplace, shopping areas); proceed to Samaria (cross-cultural ministry); and then go to the ends of the earth (international missions).

The essential steps are to—
• pray;
• see the need;
• establish a plan;
• go meet the need.

1   Identify at least one immediate ministry need that corresponds to each of the four areas mentioned in Acts 1:8.
Jerusalem: _____
Judea: _____
Samaria: _____
Ends of the earth: _____

Take a moment to commit each ministry need to Christ in prayer.

Acts 1:10 tells us that after Jesus ascended into heaven, the disciples stood gazing into heaven rather than going about their ministry. Unfortunately, it is no different today. Often Christians would rather stay in the church singing and fellowshipping than go out and serve others.

I sometimes wonder what would happen if the "two men in white clothes" (v. 10) visited our congregations today. They might say something like "Listen up, church. Why are you just standing there? Jesus will return someday, but in the meantime your job is to go … now!" The gospel was not given to the church to hide from the unsaved world. On the contrary, since we know Christ is coming back someday, we must urgently serve and share while we can.

② **Read John 4:36-38 in the margin. Circle words designating jobs people carry out in the harvest.**

③ **This week's memory verse, John 4:35, also relates to the harvest. Try writing it here from memory.**

_____

_____

John 4:36-38
"The reaper is already receiving pay and gathering fruit for eternal life, so the sower and reaper can rejoice together. For in this case the saying is true: 'One sows and another reaps.' I sent you to reap what you didn't labor for; others have labored, and you have benefited from their labor."

Understanding the principles of the harvest is imperative to fulfilling your ministry plan.
1. Plow the ground through prayer. Saturate the ministry field by praying for unsaved friends, neighbors, family, and acquaintances.
2. Plant the gospel seed. This is why servanthood is so important. Every encounter that shows the love and message of Christ will plant a seed. The more seeds you plant, the greater the potential harvest.
3. Pray and be patient. The Holy Spirit will bring the harvest.

Plow, plant, pray, and be patient. If you work the fields, the Holy Spirit will bring about the harvest in due time.

My Observation Journal

↕ Read "Community Prayerwalking" on page 100. This week walk through your Jerusalem—your immediate home, neighborhood, work, or school—and pray for needs in the area. Ask at least two persons for prayer needs. Be faithful to pray for the requests; then follow up the next day about the needs. Be sensitive to other opportunities to serve and share. Record responses in the margin.

↕ **Watch and Pray**
Pray for strength and boldness to go and serve in Christ's name.

Day 5 • Completing the Task

God's Word for Today

"Many Samaritans from that town believed in Him because of what the woman said when she testified, 'He told me everything I ever did.' Therefore, when the Samaritans came to Him, they asked Him to stay with them, and He stayed there two days. Many more believed because of what He said. And they told the woman, 'We no longer believe because of what you said, for we have heard for ourselves and know that this really is the Savior of the world.'" John 4:39–42

Read and meditate on "God's Word for Today" in the margin and spend a moment in prayer as you begin today's lesson.

I (David) was in New Orleans in the summer of 2007 working with a rebuilding project. Numerous families took their vacation time to team with Project Noah and help rebuild homes after Hurricane Katrina.

The devastation and pain were unbelievable. I will never forget the encounter with a young mother who was obviously guarded and a bit skeptical of our motives. She later shared that her husband used their floating refrigerator to drift his family to safety on the rising water.

Moved by her story and the fact that she had to purchase ice every morning to keep food from spoiling, several families sacrificed their own resources and purchased a new refrigerator for the woman. They also repaired and painted her home.

In further conversations the woman, though grateful, made several convicting observations. She first noted that numerous teams had worked in her neighborhood over the past year and had been aware of her predicament. Why had it taken so long for someone to respond? She also implied that some people had treated her family as if they were unclean. Unfortunately, she felt like a toy that people had played with and then set aside.

The difference finally came when Christians stopped long enough to empathize with her needs. In the end she and her family came to Christ!

This is exactly what happened with Jesus and the woman in John 4. It wasn't until Jesus cared enough to stop, listen, empathize, and respond to her needs that she was transformed by Christ's message.

1) Read John 4:7-42 in your Bible. Note the progression of stopping, listening, empathizing, and responding.

How long did Jesus stay with the Samaritans at their request?

_____

What was the result of Jesus' stay? _____

_____

Because Jesus stayed with the Samaritans for two days, many more believed. They testified to the Samaritan woman, "We no longer believe because of what you said, for we have heard for ourselves and know that this really is the Savior of the world" (v. 42). For our ministry to make an eternal difference, we have to be willing to stay, follow through, and ultimately complete the task of bringing the person into a personal relationship with God through Christ.

(2) **Check the statement or statements that best describe you.**
○ I have treated others carelessly by not following through and completing my ministry with them.
○ I am willing to be involved in the lives of hurting people and to stay as long as ministry is needed.

(3) **Read John 10:14-15. Circle the word *know** every time it is used.**

Unlike other world religions, Christianity is about living a personal relationship with God. How does it make you feel to know that Christ wants to know you, even as He knows His Father?

_____

Because Christ is our example, we as His disciples should seek to genuinely know hurting people in our spheres of influence as we lead them to know the Good Shepherd as well.

(4) **Read John 21:15-17 in your Bible. This passage records Jesus' first instructions to Peter after he had denied Christ. Note the healing words and Jesus' call for Peter to serve others in His name.**

Jesus asked Peter whether he was willing to fully commit his life to the task of serving Christ by serving others. Are you ready to do the same? Begin today by seeing, serving, and staying until the task is complete.

↕ **Pray about your willingness to make ministry a daily lifestyle through which you meet needs and introduce others to Jesus. Record in the margin any commitment you are willing to make.**

John 10:14-15
"I am the good shepherd. I know My own sheep, and they know Me, as the Father knows Me, and I know the Father. I lay down My life for the sheep."

* The biblical meaning of *know* is much deeper than recognition or acquaintance. It carries the idea of deep intimacy, as in marriage.

My Commitment

↕ **Watch and Pray**
Pray for strength and commitment to complete the ministry tasks God has for you.

Session 3 • Assessing Ministry Needs, Impacting Hurting People

Opening Prayer

Learning Goal

You will—
  • identify places where needs exist;
  • learn what the Bible says about assessing and meeting needs;
  • discover ways Jesus responded to people in need;
  • identify simple ways to meet needs;
  • adopt a lifestyle of meeting needs on a daily basis.

Reviewing Week 3

1. In pairs or triads take turns reciting your Scripture-memory verse, John 4:35. Discuss what it means to open your eyes and see the harvest.

2. Identify the five steps in assessing ministry needs that were presented this week (going, assessing, developing a plan, implementing, and completing). Define each step and give personal examples when you have ministered in these ways. What step is most difficult for you?

3. How does Jesus' example in John 4:5-9 illustrate His willingness to go where the needs are in spite of social taboos? Are there "Samaritan" areas of prejudice in your life? Who are the objects of this prejudice?

4. Read Matthew 9:12 and Luke 19:10. Share and discuss responses to activities 2–5 on pages 38–39.

5. Share experiences meeting lost persons' needs (p. 39). Stop and pray for God to open the doors for ministry in each of these opportunities.

6. Examine the way Jesus assessed the Samaritan woman's spiritual need in John 4:10-15. Contrast the disciples' response in verses 27-35.

7. How well do you know lost persons in your circles of influence? Name one significant personal fact about an unsaved neighbor, coworker, or family member. What can you do to be more alert to their needs?

8. Name examples of occasions when Jesus emphathized with the needs of others. How can you emphathize with others as you minister?

9. Identify the ministry needs you identified in your home, workplace, or neighborhood (prayer activity, p. 41). Share your experience in meeting a need for a stranger.

10. Review the SERVE acrostic for developing a ministry plan (p. 43). Share any plans you developed and implemented this week.

11. Read Acts 1:8 and share responses to activity 1 on page 44. Do you have difficulty putting ministry plans to work? Why?

12. Read John 4:36-38. Discuss the principles of the harvest on page 45. Who plows? Who plants? Who brings the harvest? Share your experiences in prayerwalking and engaging persons in your Jerusalem.

13. Beyond going, assessing needs, developing a ministry plan, and implementing the plan, what does it mean to complete the task? Share any commitments you made to develop a lifestyle of ministry (p. 47).

Ministering to Others

1. Share ideas for discovering ministry needs and carrying out ministry plans. Start with these.
   - Go door to door and ask whether residents have prayer requests. You can do the same with a waiter or a store clerk.
   - Prayerwalk through your neighborhood, praying for each household, with the goal of meeting physical and spiritual needs. Review the suggestions in "Community Prayerwalking," page 100.
   - Map out your neighborhood or workplace. Fill in the names of family members as you get acquainted. Pray over the map daily.
   - After praying over your spheres of influence, follow up by surprising neighbors and friends with a treat, mow their grass, rake leaves, or offer to baby-sit.

2. Examine "My Ministry List" on page 92. How have you assessed needs and implemented ministry plans this week? Who needs to be added?

3. Commit to one act of service for a neighbor during the next week.

Praying Together

In small groups pray for the following.
   - Pray by name for neighbors to whom you have committed to minister and for persons on your ministry lists.
   - Pray that God will give you a willingness to reach out and meet needs, empathetic eyes to see needs, and a ministry plan for persons in your circles of relationship.

Previewing Week 4

Turn to page 51 and preview the study for the coming week.

Week 4

Networking at Church
to Extend Your Reach

"Two are better than one because they
have a good reward for their efforts."
Ecclesiastes 4:9

Networking at Church to Extend Your Reach

Phil Butler was leading a workshop on partnering in ministry. After the session he saw a man weeping. Expecting that the man had experienced a great tragedy, Butler offered a handkerchief. "Are you alright?" he asked. Butler was surprised when the man explained that these were tears of joy. "I've finally seen how my life fits into the whole picture of God's work here. For the first time in my life, I see that I have a real role along with others in God's plan."[1] When you minister to others, you don't have to work alone. You can join hands with others to have a greater impact for the Kingdom.

LEARNING GOALS
This week you will—
• describe the Kingdom impact believers can have by ministering together;
• identify the strategic role of the church in meeting ministry needs;
• recognize the importance of connecting acts of ministry with the good news;
• learn how God has wired you to minister with other believers;
• discover ways to network with others to extend your ministry reach.

OVERVIEW OF WEEK 4
Day 1: The Impact of Working Together
Day 2: It All Begins at Church
Day 3: Connecting Good Works and Good News
Day 4: Uniquely You
Day 5: Get on Board!

VERSE TO MEMORIZE
Ecclesiastes 4:9

DISCIPLESHIP HELPS FOR WEEK 4
My Ministry List (p. 92)
Equipped to SERVE (pp. 101–3)
My SERVE Profile (p. 104)
Community Organizations and Agencies (p. 105)

1. Phil Butler, *Well Connected: Releasing Power and Restoring Hope Through Kingdom Partnerships*
    (Waynesboro, GA: Authentic, 2005), 10.

Day 1 • The Impact of Working Together

God's Word for Today

"What is Apollos? And what is Paul? They are servants through whom you believed, and each has the role the Lord has given. I planted, Apollos watered, but God gave the growth. So then neither the one who plants nor the one who waters is anything, but only God who gives the growth. Now the one who plants and the one who waters are equal, and each will receive his own reward according to his own labor. For we are God's co-workers. You are God's field, God's building. According to God's grace that was given to me, as a skilled master builder I have laid a foundation, and another builds on it. But each one must be careful how he builds on it."
1 Corinthians 3:5-10

↕ Read and meditate on "God's Word for Today" in the margin and spend a moment in prayer as you begin today's lesson.

In the weeks after the flood waters receded in New Orleans after hurricane Katrina, I (Richard) met with association, church, and civic leaders to address the fact that 606 churches of all denominations were not functioning and that most of the 903 functioning churches were operating in other locations with only part of their membership. The Lord gave us a plan to divide the area south of Lake Pontchartrain into 27 areas. Southern Baptist Convention partners would become area managers and would work with the churches in a specific area to rebuild church buildings, homes, and lives.

Eight Southern Baptist state conventions and New Orleans Baptist Theological Seminary took responsibility for the seven most heavily damaged areas. Operation Noah Rebuild, the Baptist CrossRoads Project, and other ministries brought volunteers to the other areas. Through this partnership, volunteer organizations did what God had designed each to do and did together what they could not do independently. As a result, thousands of volunteers were deployed in a strategic manner to make a real difference.

1 **Identify a time when you or your church ministered with others.**

_____

2 **Reread 1 Corinthians 3:5-10 in the margin. Write *T* for *true* or *F* for *false* beside the following statements.**
___ a. You are responsible for the salvation of lost individuals.
___ b. Evangelism is better viewed as a process, not an event.
___ c. No individual role in bringing people to faith in Christ is of greater value than another.
___ d. All of your efforts have no effect if God doesn't act.
___ e. Your contribution to the salvation process is not of your own doing; it is a gift from God.
___ f. God will reward those who share the gospel.
___ g. You must be careful to minister effectively.
___ h. What you contribute to the evangelism process through ministry to others impacts the effectiveness of others.

Answers: a-F, b-T, c-T, d-T, e-T, f-T, g-T, h-T

Paul's vision for ministry involves many people in serving others with the gifts God has given them. Although each person plays a different role in the process, all work for the common goal of bringing others to a knowledge of Christ. Nevertheless, all results come from God. We are coworkers with Him, but only He "gives the growth" (v. 7).

(3) **Read Ecclesiastes 4:7-12 in the margin. Check the things you can expect when you work with others.**
- ○ Support
- ○ Distraction
- ○ Mutual benefit
- ○ Futility
- ○ Freedom to do things your way
- ○ Strength
- ○ A good reward
- ○ Other: _____

This week's memory verse comes from this passage. Write verse 9 here.

_____

_____

Working with others in ministry provides greater strength, focus, and support. Consider the greater impact you can make by ministering with others in the body of Christ.

Last week you began to assess needs around you and to respond to ministry opportunities God had given to you. This week you will look for opportunities to network with someone who is serving others.

(4) **Today join a family member who routinely provides a service to your family and talk with him or her about the way God designed us to serve others.**

If you live alone, look for an opportunity at work to help someone complete a project. Talk to him or her about the value of doing things together.

Use "My Observation Journal" in the margin to record the person's response, what God said to you through this experience, and what you are going to do in response.

Pray about your current ministry involvement. Do you need to bring others into your ministry or join someone else in ministry?

Ecclesiastes 4:7-12

"[7]I saw futility under the sun: [8]There is a person without a companion, without even a son or brother, and though there is no end to all his struggles, his eyes are still not content with riches. 'So who am I struggling for,' he asks, 'and depriving myself from good?' This too is futile and a miserable task. [9]Two are better than one because they have a good reward for their efforts. [10]For if either falls, his companion can lift him up; but pity the one who falls without another to lift him up. [11]Also, if two lie down together, they can keep warm; but how can one person alone keep warm? [12]And if somebody overpowers one person, two can resist him. A cord of three strands is not easily broken."

My Observation Journal

Day 2 • It All Begins at Church

↕ Read and meditate on "God's Word for Today" in the margin and spend a moment in prayer as you begin today's lesson.

Before God called me (Richard) to preach, our family was part of a great church in Louisiana. I was the director of a Young Adult Sunday School department that presented many opportunities to minister to others. We had an expanding list of families to connect with who were not part of our church, as well as opportunities to meet needs and share Christ with the family members of persons in our department.

I recall one member whose husband was not a church member. Mike had cancer, so I regularly visited him in the hospital and read to him from the Bible. He was often in great pain, and the words of Scripture seemed to bring him comfort. If not for my church and my Sunday School department, I would not have had the opportunity to serve Mike in Jesus' name.

① **Review Acts 13:1-3 in the margin and answer these questions.**
What types of leaders had God placed in the church at Antioch?

_____

What were these leaders doing when the Holy Spirit spoke?

_____

Whom did the Holy Spirit select for a particular ministry?

_____

Acts 13:1-3 teaches us at least four things about the impact of the local church in ministering to others.
1. God places leaders in the body of Christ (see v. 1).
2. In the local church we connect to other believers for ministry (see v. 2a).
3. The Holy Spirit looks in the church to identify individuals to carry out new ministry (see v. 2b).
4. The church is the agent for advancing new ministry to others (see v. 3).

Ephesians 4:11-12 tells us that God places leaders in the body to equip the members for the work of service that leads to the building up of the body.

God is a God of presence. When Jesus was on earth, He was present as God in the flesh. Because Jesus now lives in His people, the church is God's expression of Himself on earth. Not all ministry settings have a direct church connection, but wherever you see a need—at work, in the community, or among your family and friends—you are God's means of putting these persons in contact with the body of Christ. Because you are part of the body, you can marshal the church's resources to meet specific needs.

2) **What ministry resources does the body of Christ provide that you cannot provide alone?**

_____

Your church can provide people—people to pray, to join you in ministry, to hold you accountable, to provide material resources you don't have, and to connect with individuals as they respond to Jesus Christ. You don't have to minister alone, nor did God intend for you to.

3) **Identify ministry actions sponsored by your church that allow members to serve one another.**

_____

4) **Identify ministry actions sponsored by your church that allow members to serve people in the community.**

_____

5) **How much does your church do to equip the body to minister?**
○ Very little   ○ Occasional training   ○ Consistent equipping

6) **How often does your church involve members in ministry?**
○ Rarely   ○ Occasionally   ○ Frequently

7) **With whom in your church can you network to minister to someone this week? What will you do to minister together this week? To whom will you minister?**

_____

Update "My Ministry List" on page 92 after you have ministered. Use "My Observation Journal" in the margin to record the response to your ministry.

> Because you are part of the body, you can marshal the church's resources to meet specific needs.

My Observation Journal

Day 3 • Connecting Good Works and Good News

↕ Read and meditate on "God's Word for Today" in the margin
and spend a moment in prayer as you begin today's lesson.

God's Word for Today

"In Lystra a man without strength in his feet, lame from birth, and who had never walked, sat and heard Paul speaking. After observing him closely and seeing that he had faith to be healed, Paul said in a loud voice, 'Stand up straight on your feet!' And he jumped up and started to walk around. When the crowds saw what Paul had done, they raised their voices, saying in the Lycaonian language, 'The gods have come down to us in the form of men!' The apostles Barnabas and Paul tore their robes when they heard this and rushed into the crowd, shouting: 'Men! Why are you doing these things? We are men also, with the same nature as you, and we are proclaiming good news to you, that you should turn from these worthless things to the living God, who made the heaven, the earth, the sea, and everything in them.'"
Acts 14:8-11,14-16

In July 2006 Jim Shankula, the border-ministry coordinator for Shadow Mountain Community Church, led a group of 12 volunteers to participate in Feeding Those Who Feed Us, a ministry to migrant workers sponsored by the California Baptist Convention. The staff at Shadow Mountain had been praying about how the church's participation would fit into its strategic plan to reach people with the gospel through missions around the world.

After receiving assurance that evangelism would be connected to the acts of kindness and that a Hispanic church close to the migrant camp would follow up with those who were reached, the church joined the state's effort. When Shadow Mountain worked with other churches to connect good works and good news, the people in the migrant camp were moved by the unconditional love shown by the team and by God's Word. Seventy-one invited Jesus to come into their lives.

Ministry is incomplete if it doesn't lead to a communication of the gospel. When you meet someone's physical needs, always be ready to introduce them to Jesus, the only One who can meet their spiritual needs.

① **Refer to "God's Word for Today" in the margin and check the things Paul did to meet the man's need.**
○ Assessed his need   ○ Shared the gospel   ○ Healed him

Paul did all of these things and more! Paul's example provides a pattern for connecting good works and good news.
• Paul came near (see v. 9).
• Paul observed the man and assessed his need (see v. 9).
• Paul invited the man to take a step of faith and met a need (see v. 10).
• Paul connected the gospel to the ministry (see vv. 14-16).

A story is told about retired professional baseball player Hank Aaron. During a crucial game the catcher of the opposing team attempted to distract Hank's attention by carrying on an unusual amount of conversation.

Not having much luck, the catcher said, "Hank, you have the bat turned wrong. You can't read the label." He kept up the chatter about the label for several pitches until Hank hit the ball out of the park. After rounding the bases and crossing home plate, Hank said to the catcher, "I didn't come here to read."

Always keep in mind the reason you are ministering. Are you using the opportunity to invite someone to consider the good news? When ministering to others, always ask these three questions.

1. How do you connect the gospel to your intentional acts of kindness? Believing in Christ is the ultimate goal.
2. How do you connect new believers to the body of Christ? Becoming a member of the local body means new believers have to make a commitment and the local body of Christ has to accept them into the family.
3. How do you engage new believers in ministry to others in their community? This may be the most difficult of the three because it requires participation in the fellowship and involves the new believer in the life of the church outside the four walls.

2) **Assess the way you and your church make these connections. Place a number in each blank, with 1 being ineffective and 5 being effective.**

	You	Your Church
Connecting ministry to the gospel	___	___
Connecting new believers to the body	___	___
Engaging new believers in ministry	___	___

James 1:22 reminds us that communicating the gospel involves both word and deed. Acting and speaking complement each other. Serving is to acting as a complete gospel presentation is to speaking. Acting without serving is incomplete, and speaking without getting to the truth about Jesus Christ is incomplete.

3) **During the past three weeks you have made service your vehicle for ministry. Now make sure you connect individuals to Jesus. Start practicing the three-step outline on this page. Use "My Observation Journal" in the margin to record what you discover this week. Update "My Ministry List" on page 92 when you minister or share the gospel.**

4) **Practice saying this week's memory verse, Ecclesiastes 4:9, out loud.**

James 1:22
"Be doers of the word and not hearers only."

My Observation Journal

Watch and Pray
As you become more intentional about sharing Christ when you minister, also be more intentional about praying as you approach ministry opportunities. Pray that God will open the person's eyes to see Jesus in your actions and will open their heart to receive the good news.

Day 4 • Uniquely You

· · · · · · · · · · · · · · · · · · · ·

God's Word for Today

"The body is one and has many parts, and all the parts of that body, though many, are one body—so also is Christ. For we were all baptized by one Spirit into one body—whether Jews or Greeks, whether slaves or free—and we were all made to drink of one Spirit. So the body is not one part but many. But now God has placed the parts, each one of them, in the body just as He wanted. So the eye cannot say to the hand, 'I don't need you!' nor again the head to the feet, 'I don't need you!' On the contrary, all the more, those parts of the body that seem to be weaker are necessary.
1 Corinthians 12:12-14,18,21-22

Read and meditate on "God's Word for Today" in the margin and spend a moment in prayer as you begin today's lesson.

In the movie *The Rookie* the main character, Jim Morris, wrestles with the disappointment of an unsatisfied life. The movie is the true-life account of Texas high-school chemistry teacher and baseball coach Jim Morris, whose lifetime ambition to play professional ball returns in the form of his dormant fastball. He is torn between his love for his family and his desire to fulfill his dreams. The drama that weaves itself through the movie is captured emotionally in the disconnect that exists between Morris and the people who mean the most to him as he pursues his ambition.

As Morris works through his decision about returning to the major league, he seeks affirmation from his estranged father. It comes in a very tense scene when his father releases him by saying, "It's OK to do what you want to do, but there comes a time to do what you were meant to do."

1. **Review "God's Word for Today" in the margin and fill in the blanks.**
   a. There is _____ body but _____ parts.
   b. We were baptized by one _____ into one body.
   c. _____ has placed the parts in the body just as He wanted.
   d. All of the parts of the body are _____.

Although the body of Christ is one, it is composed of many parts, just like the human body. God places the parts in the body of Christ according to His purposes. This means in fulfilling the mission of the church, God has prepared a place for you and you for a place. He has a purpose He wants you to fulfill through the body in which He has placed you. Do you know what you were meant to do as part of the body of Christ?

2. **Completing the following inventory will give you insight into the way God has wired you for ministry through His body.**

When you have unrestricted time, how do you normally choose to spend it?

_____

Answers: a. one, many;
b. Spirit; c. God; d. necessary

When given a choice, which would you rather do?
○ Interact with people
○ Do something on your own
○ Direct others to do things

What one thing can you do that someone else might ask you to teach them to do?

_____

Is there a particular group of individuals with whom it seems natural for you to interact? If so, who are they?

_____

What skills come naturally to you? _____

_____

Do you have resources you are willing to use for the benefit of others?

_____

When you meet people for the first time, do you wonder
about their relationship with Jesus Christ?   ○ Yes   ○ No
Do you regularly set aside time to pray for people?   ○ Yes   ○ No
Do you find it easy to tell someone about changes
God is leading you to make in your life?   ○ Yes   ○ No

③ Read "Equipped to SERVE" and "My SERVE Profile" on pages 101–4. Plan to use the recommended tools to learn more about your gifts, skills, and passion.

④ In the margin identify opportunities you have to minister with others. These may be ministries promoted by your church, needs you identified earlier in this study, or ideas in "Community Organizations and Agencies" on page 105. For each ministry you list in the margin, check the feature that attracts you to it—an ability you have; your passion; the leader; or its strategic nature, that is, something that needs to be done. Select the ministry you would most like to meet by networking with one or more believers. Enlist these individuals and carry out the ministry. Record the results in "My Observation Journal" in the margin. Remember to update "My Ministry List" when you minister.

Potential Ministry Opportunities

Ministry: _____
○ Ability
○ Passion
○ Individual leading
○ Strategic

Ministry: _____
○ Ability
○ Passion
○ Individual leading
○ Strategic

Ministry: _____
○ Ability
○ Passion
○ Individual leading
○ Strategic

My Observation Journal

Watch and Pray
Spend time in prayer with the ministry partner(s) you have enlisted.

Day 5 • Get on Board!

⇕ Read and meditate on "God's Word for Today" in the margin
and spend a moment in prayer as you begin today's lesson.

Experience in the mission of the church draws others to work in the mission. Avery Willis once said to me (Richard), "When I first began to write discipleship material, the model for involvement followed this pattern: read about it, have feelings about it, and then experience it. The model has changed to: experience it, have feelings about it, and possibly want to read about it."

Whether you are actively ministering to others by serving them or you are still thinking about it, the objective for this week is to join someone who is currently serving others. If this is a first for you, a partner will make it easier for you to adopt someone else's problem as your problem. If you are currently engaged in ministry, you need to experience what it is like joining someone who is doing it. In both instances God wants to teach you something and bring some changes in your life.

1 **Change is what Acts 11 is all about. Reread "God's Word for Today" and underline the occasions when someone faced a change.**

Remember two things about the changes you identified in Acts 11:
1. A group of people received the gospel who previously had no access.
2. Two men worked together to take the gospel to them.

2 **Write the name of the group who received the gospel.**

_____

Write the names of the men. _____

_____

Identify some changes God has brought in your life since you started ministering to others.

_____

_____

_____

God's Word for Today

"The apostles and the brothers who were throughout Judea heard that the Gentiles had welcomed God's message also. When Peter went up to Jerusalem, those who stressed circumcision argued with him, saying, 'You visited uncircumcised men and ate with them!' Peter began to explain to them in an orderly sequence. When they heard this they became silent. Then they glorified God, saying, 'So God has granted repentance resulting in life to even the Gentiles!' Those who had been scattered as a result of the persecution that started with Stephen made their way to Phoenicia, Cyprus, and Antioch, speaking the message to no one except the Jews. But there were some of them, Cypriot and Cyrenian men, who came to Antioch and began speaking to the Hellenists, proclaiming the good news about the Lord Jesus. The Lord's hand was with them, and a large number who believed turned to the Lord. Then he [Barnabas] went to Tarsus to search for Saul, and when he had found him he brought him

Not everyone wants to make immediate changes. There are always early adopters, middle adopters, late adopters, and never adopters.[1] So where are you in the matter of ministry to others?

3. **Check your predominant reaction to the idea of networking with other believers to minister. Does the prospect of joining someone in order to serve others—**
   ○ excite you?   ○ make you anxious?
   ○ convict you?   ○ fulfill you?
   ○ Other: _____

The fact that you are reading and applying this material indicates that you are ready to act.

4. **In week 1 you observed persons who are serving others. Write the names of believers God might want you to join with to minister to someone.**

   _____

   _____

↕ **Read Psalm 5:1-3 in the margin. David laid his requests before God on a daily basis and then waited for God to answer. Spend time in prayer asking God to—**
   • show you where He wants you to join someone in ministry;
   • give you boldness to talk to the individual today;
   • show you what you need to do to get started.

As we said earlier, experience in the mission of the church draws others to work in the mission. As you work with others in the body of Christ, you will be able to do far more for the Kingdom than you could alone.

5. **Record your memory verse for this week, Ecclesiastes 4:9.**

   _____

   _____

6. **What differences have you observed when ministering with others that you haven't experienced when ministering alone? Record your response in "My Observation Journal" in the margin.**

to Antioch. For a whole year they met with the church and taught large numbers, and the disciples were first called Christians in Antioch."
Acts 11:1-4,18-21,25-26

Psalm 5:1-3
"Listen to my words, LORD; consider my sighing. Pay attention to the sound of my cry, my King and my God, for I pray to You. At daybreak, LORD, You hear my voice; at daybreak I plead my case to You and watch expectantly."

My Observation Journal

1. Aubrey Malphurs, *Pouring New Wine into Old Wineskins* (Grand Rapids: Baker, 1993), 100–106.

Session 4 • Networking at Church to Extend Your Reach

Opening Prayer

Learning Goals
You will—

- describe the Kingdom impact believers can have by ministering together;
- identify the strategic role of the church in meeting ministry needs;
- recognize the importance of connecting acts of ministry with the good news;
- learn how God has wired you to minister with other believers;
- discover ways to network with others to extend your ministry reach.

Reviewing Week 4

1. In pairs or triads take turns reciting your Scripture-memory verse, Ecclesiastes 4:9. What implications does this verse have for ministry to others? What are the rewards for your effort?

2. Read 1 Corinthians 3:5-10. Share and discuss answers to the true/false activity (activity 2) on page 52. Identify various roles that might contribute to someone's decision to accept Jesus as Savior and Lord. Is any role in the body of Christ more important than any other? Who actually brings someone to a knowledge of Christ?

3. How can the body of Christ provide more effective ministry than an individual can? Give examples of ways your church ministers together.

4. Read Acts 13:1-3 and review the numbered statements at the bottom of page 54. In what ways does the church embody God's presence in the world? How faithfully does your church do that?

5. Discuss how much of your church's ministry is directed to church members and how much is directed to the lost community.

6. Why is it so important to connect acts of ministry with a clear communication of the gospel? How did Paul do that in Acts 14:8-16?

7. Review the three questions on page 57. Share your answers to activity 2 on that page to evaluate how you and your church connect ministry to the gospel, connect new believers to the body, and engage new believers in ministry. Give examples of any ways you have done these things.

8. Read 1 Corinthians 12:12-22 and share your answers to activity 1 on page 58. How does your church demonstrate that every member of the body is important?

9. Share the results of the inventory you completed on pages 58–59 (activity 2). What are the implications for the way you network with other believers to minister?

10. What did you learn about your gifts and skills for ministry from "Equipped to SERVE" (pp. 101–3) and "My SERVE Profile" (p. 104)?

11. What ministries did you identify on page 59 that you would like to participate in? Why were you drawn to these? How are you uniquely designed for these? Is there a particular ministry you feel God is calling you to? If you had to identify a ministry God meant for you to do, what would it be?

12. Discuss this statement: "Experience in the mission of the church draws others to work in the mission" (p. 60). Are you ready to join other believers to minister? If so, what do you need to do as a first step? If you are not ready, what changes are needed to position you for ministry?

Ministering to Others

1. Share the results of the ministry action you committed to in the previous group session (p. 49). Were you able to share the gospel?

2. Share any ministry partners you have joined with this week in ministry. What were the results? How did people respond to your ministry? What was different about being involved with another believer in ministry?

3. Review "Community Organizations and Agencies" on page 105. Which might be suitable for you or your church to partner with in ministry?

Praying Together

1. Pray for individuals on your ministry list who have been mentioned.

2. Pray for participants in these ways.
   • God's direction as participants seek the ministries
     He has equipped them to fulfill
   • Ministry partners and particular avenues of ministry
   • Any uncertainties participants have expressed about
     ministering with other believers
   • The filling of the Spirit as participants move out in ministry

Previewing Week 5

Turn to page 65 and preview the study for the coming week.

Week 5

Drawing Near
to Christ

"Go, therefore, and make disciples
of all nations, baptizing them in the name
of the Father and of the Son and of the
Holy Spirit, teaching them to observe
everything I have commanded you.
And remember, I am with you always,
to the end of the age."
Matthew 28:19–20

Drawing Near to Christ

The Great Commission cannot be done at a distance; it requires you to go near the persons who need ministry. You have to be willing to serve them by entering their world and expending your resources to meet their needs. Doing less will limit your ministry. So far in this study you have observed people ministering to others, you have identified opportunities for ministry around you, and you have joined others in ministry. This week you will go near those who need your ministry. To go near others effectively, you must also draw near to God.

LEARNING GOALS

This week you will—
• explain why abiding in Christ is essential to ministry;
• recognize the importance of listening to Jesus before ministering;
• define what it means to be a neighbor to someone in need;
• learn principles for announcing the coming of God's kingdom;
• identify ways to stay connected to God when ministering to others.

OVERVIEW OF WEEK 5

Day 1: Abide in the Vine
Day 2: Listen Before You Minister
Day 3: Become the Neighbor They Need
Day 4: The Kingdom on Your Doorstep
Day 5: The God You Can't Ignore

VERSES TO MEMORIZE

Matthew 28:19-20

DISCIPLESHIP HELPS FOR WEEK 5

My Ministry List (p. 92)
Kingdom-Coming Principles (p. 106)

Day 1 • Abide in the Vine

God's Word for Today

"I am the true vine, and My Father is the vineyard keeper. Every branch in Me that does not produce fruit He removes, and He prunes every branch that produces fruit so that it will produce more fruit. I am the vine; you are the branches. The one who remains in Me and I in him produces much fruit, because you can do nothing without Me. My Father is glorified by this: that you produce much fruit and prove to be My disciples."
John 15:1-2,5,8

Jesus' relationship with His Father models the abiding relationship we are to have with Him.

Read and meditate on "God's Word for Today" in the margin and spend a moment in prayer as you begin today's lesson.

I (Richard) grew up in a home that made church a priority. I was baptized at age 11 but did not come to know Jesus Christ as my personal Savior until I was a young married adult. The Lord had placed my wife and me in a church that focused on qualities that should characterize the Christian life. After several years of being around other people who demonstrated these qualities, I began to sense that something was missing in my life. I saw Christians who were developing a lifestyle of abiding in Christ, while my life failed to produce fruit.

God started by reaching my wife, and I met Jesus several weeks after that. Attention to God's Word dominated my new life. I had an insatiable desire to read and study God's Word. My wife says that many nights I would be sitting at my desk when she went to sleep, and she would awake to find me in the same position, reading and studying God's Word.

Abiding in Christ is absolutely essential for those who minister to others. Staying connected with Jesus keeps us attuned to His heart and will for our ministry. Jesus even said if we do not abide in Him, our ministry will not produce fruit.

1. **Reread "God's Word for Today" and answer these questions.**
Who is the vine? _____

Who are the branches? _____

Why is it essential to remain in Jesus? _____
_____

How does abiding in Christ bring glory to God? _____
_____

Jesus' relationship with His Father models the abiding relationship we are to have with Him.

② **Read John 5:19 in the margin. What did Jesus do on His own?**

_____

How did Jesus know when to act? _____

Just as Jesus abode in an obedient relationship with the Father, we are to remain in an obedient relationship with Him. Spending time in the Word is just one way we maintain an abiding relationship with Jesus (see John 8:31). Jesus modeled other expressions of abiding with His Father:
- Jesus demolished problems through bold prayer (see Mark 8:6-9).
- Jesus listened to the Father before making decisions (see Luke 6:12-16).
- Jesus prevailed over difficulty by trusting the Father (see Matthew 4:1-11).
- Jesus constantly obeyed the Father (see Hebrews 4:14-15).
- Jesus always pointed the way to the Father (John 14:6).

Based on Jesus' model, we can identify at least six signs of abiding:
1. Reading God's Word
2. Praying that totally depends on God
3. Seeking God's plan for serving
4. Obeying God rather than people
5. Listening to God, supported by listening to wise counsel
6. Trusting God when things around you might say otherwise

③ **Go back and circle the numbers beside the signs of abiding that characterize your life.**

When you abide in Christ, you move in His provision and at His command. Your life will then produce fruit that brings glory to the Father.

↕ **Express to God your desire to abide in Christ. Review the six signs of abiding and confess the areas in which you are weak. Ask God to enable you to abide in Him and to move out in ministry as He directs. Thank Him for His provision to minister in His name.**

④ **Write in the margin any commitments you want to make about things you will do to abide in Christ. One idea is suggested.**

⑤ **Start memorizing your memory verses for this week, Matthew 28:19-20. If you would like, tear out and use the card at the back of the book.**

John 5:19
"I assure you: The Son is not able to do anything on His own, but only what He sees the Father doing. For whatever the Father does, the Son also does these things in the same way."

John 8:31
"If you continue in My word, you really are My disciples."

My Commitments
- Learn more about abiding in Christ by studying _Growing Disciples: Abide in Christ_ (see p. 112).

Week 5 » Day 1

Day 2 • Listen Before You Minister

God's Word for Today

"While they were traveling, He entered a village, and a woman named Martha welcomed Him into her home. She had a sister named Mary, who also sat at the Lord's feet and was listening to what He said. But Martha was distracted by her many tasks, and she came up and asked, 'Lord, don't You care that my sister has left me to serve alone? So tell her to give me a hand.' The Lord answered her, 'Martha, Martha, you are worried and upset about many things, but one thing is necessary. Mary has made the right choice, and it will not be taken away from her.'"
Luke 10:38-42

Read and meditate on "God's Word for Today" in the margin and spend a moment in prayer as you begin today's lesson.

Our (Richard's) family takes a family vacation every summer. One year we opted for a houseboat on Lake Lanier near our home rather than a condo at the beach. Everyone thought, *Wow! A 54-foot-long houseboat!* I thought, *A 54-foot-long houseboat? Wow!* When the dock steward said not to worry, that he'd tell me everything I needed to know, I had a sneaky suspicion about what the week might hold.

The houseboat had no anchor. The steward instructed me to run the boat onto the beach and tie, at a 45-degree angle, to a tree or a stump. I would have to beach the houseboat perpendicular to the beach and make sure there was a 10-foot depth or more at the back. The rest of the steward's instructions were a blur.

After several attempts to land in several locations, I finally got it right. Monday, Tuesday, and Wednesday there were no problems; but Thursday afternoon brought a wind from a different direction, placing a tremendous strain on the two ropes that kept the boat in place. I had remembered to tie the ropes securely to trees and had neatly wrapped them around aluminum "horns" on the front of the boat. However, I had not heard the steward's instructions to tie off the rope on the iron cleats on the rim of the boat. I was on top of the boat lounging when I heard what sounded like the crack of a 22-caliber rifle. One of the aluminum horns had broken, and now only one rope was holding our boat on the beach.

Fortunately, nothing bad happened, and we soon got things under control; but this incident reminds me of the importance of listening before launching. Luke 10:38-42 also provides a lesson in listening.

1) **Review Luke 10:38-42 in the margin and answer these questions.**
What was Martha doing during Jesus' visit? _____
What was Mary doing? _____
How did Jesus describe Martha? _____
How did Jesus evaluate Mary's decision? _____

What do you think Mary gained by listening to Jesus? _____

_____

What do you think Martha missed by doing other things?

_____

When Mary chose listening over working, Jesus called her decision "necessary" and "the right choice" (v. 42). In effect He said to Mary, "That is a good thing. A time is coming when you'll need this information, and no one will be able to take it away from you."

Always sit at Jesus' feet before you go out to minister. You can't know how to minister until you have heard from Him. You need His compassion. You need His instruction. You need His wisdom. You need His power.

(2) **What does it mean to sit at Jesus' feet?** _____

If you make a practice of sitting at Jesus' feet, what does it imply about your relationship with Him? What impact will it have on your relationship? _____

Have you already established the practice of listening to Jesus?
○ Yes   ○ No

What obstacles keep you from sitting at Jesus' feet?

_____

_____

Check the conditions that help you listen.
○ To have no interruptions
○ To make notes on what I am hearing
○ To connect visual images with what I am hearing
○ Other: _____

Sit at Jesus' feet for 5 to 10 minutes. Don't say a thing. Listen to what He says to you about people you have encountered over the past four weeks. Use "My Observation Journal" in the margin to record what God says to you, what you are going to do about it, and what you need to ask God to do.

Always sit at Jesus' feet before you go out to minister.

My Observation Journal

Day 3 • Become the Neighbor They Need

God's Word for Today

"²⁹Wanting to justify himself, he asked Jesus, 'And who is my neighbor?' ³⁰Jesus took up the question and said: 'A man was going down from Jerusalem to Jericho and fell into the hands of robbers. They stripped him, beat him up, and fled, leaving him half dead. ³¹A priest happened to be going down that road. When he saw him, he passed by on the other side. ³²In the same way, a Levite, when he arrived at the place and saw him, passed by on the other side. ³³But a Samaritan on his journey came up to him, and when he saw the man, he had compassion. ³⁴He went over to him and bandaged his wounds, pouring on oil and wine. Then he put him on his own animal, brought him to an inn, and took care of him. ³⁵The next day he took out two denarii, gave them to the innkeeper, and said, "Take care of him. When I come back I'll reimburse you for whatever extra you spend." ³⁶Which of these three do you think proved to be a neighbor to the man who fell into the hands of the robbers?' ³⁷'The one who showed mercy to him,' he said. Then Jesus told him, 'Go and do the same.'" Luke 10:29–37

Read and meditate on "God's Word for Today" in the margin and spend a moment in prayer as you begin today's lesson.

There weren't many neighbors in Lynch, Kentucky, when God led Lonnie and Belinda Riley to return to their roots. Thirty years earlier the Rileys had left rural central Appalachia in search of a better life as the coal-mining industry went bust in this once affluent region. The region has made progress; but Harlan County, where the Rileys now live, is the most economically depressed area in Kentucky. The unemployment rate stands at about 35 percent, while the high-school dropout rate is 40 percent. "There are not a lot of jobs here," says Lonnie, a former engineer and retired pastor. "When we came back here, there was no hope. Our message has been: where there is Jesus, there is hope."

Upon their return to Lynch, the Rileys soon realized that actions really do speak louder than words. After six months of praying and trying to reacquaint themselves with the neighbors, Lonnie purchased a pair of hedge-cutting shears and worked lot by lot sprucing up the overgrown community by offering free landscaping services. A few months later, the couple distributed about six thousand homemade sugar cookies, again going door to door, to wish their neighbors a Merry Christmas. "When you eat those cookies, remember that Jesus loves you, and this is a great season to celebrate that," the Rileys encouraged their new neighbors.

The Rileys say they are living proof that you don't have to be wealthy to care for those who have great physical and spiritual needs. Summers have become a great opportunity for volunteers to come near the individuals who live in the area, but the ministries are now year-round. As the Rileys and the volunteers serve, many people hear and see the gospel, and they are making professions of faith in Jesus Christ.

The Rileys demonstrate the gospel in word and deed. They returned to Lynch because they were listening to God and were obedient when He told them to act.[1] Now that you have begun to listen to God and to watch what He is doing around you, it is time for you to act as well. To whom does God want you to be a neighbor?

From Luke 10:29-37 we learn that a neighbor is someone—
• whom others have taken advantage of (see v. 30);
• whom others are ignoring (see vv. 31-32);
• who is in your path (see v. 33);
• for whom you have compassion (see v. 33);
• who needs resources you have (see vv. 34-35).

① **Refer to "God's Word for Today" as you answer these questions.**
How had the man been taken advantage of? _____
Who ignored the man? _____
Who felt compassion and responded to the man? _____
What resources did he provide to care for the man?

_____

Over the past several months I (Richard) have visited a jail in our community. As I have met inmates' family and friends, I have felt compassion and prayed for them. I have continued to visit one inmate the Lord put on my heart. At the end of my latest visit, the individual prayed, "God, thank You for my friend Richard." I have become his neighbor.

Your neighbor could be someone whose arms are full and needs assistance to open a door. It could be your child who needs assistance with homework. It could be a neighbor who needs help around the house. It could be a person you pass on the street who needs a smile or a thank-you.

② **As you read at the top of this page the criteria of a neighbor, whom does God bring to mind for you to be a neighbor to? Record their names on "My Ministry List," page 92. What do you need to do to meet their need?**

_____

_____

Read "Relational-Evangelism Skills" in the margin. Pray about becoming the neighbor someone needs.

③ **Review in the margin the five ministry actions you learned in week 1. Use "My Observation Journal" in the margin to record what God is saying to you about becoming a neighbor in these ways.**

Relational-Evangelism Skills

1. The awareness of opportunity (attentiveness to opportunities to witness while you are in the situation)
2. A Christlike attitude
3. Attentive body language
4. Tone of voice
5. The ability to start a conversation and keep it going
6. Directive questioning (the ability to ask questions that steer the conversation toward spiritual matters)
7. Active listening

Five Ministry Actions

1. Bridge building
2. Offering relief
3. Interceding
4. Offering hospitality
5. Promoting spiritual growth

My Observation Journal

1. See Henry Blackaby, Richard Blackaby, and Claude King, *Experiencing God Leader Kit* (Nashville: LifeWay Press, 2007), DVD 5, for testimonies from Lynch, Kentucky.

God's Word for Today

"After this the Lord appointed 70 others, and He sent them ahead of Him in pairs to every town and place where He Himself was about to go. He told them: 'The harvest is abundant, but the workers are few. Therefore, pray to the Lord of the harvest to send out workers into His harvest. Now go; I'm sending you out like lambs among wolves. Don't carry a money-bag, traveling bad, or sandals; don't greet anyone along the road. Whatever house you enter, first say, "Peace to this household." If a son of peace is there, your peace will rest on him; but if not, it will return to you. Remain in the same house, eating and drinking what they offer, for the worker is worthy of his wages. Don't be moving from house to house. When you enter any town, and they welcome you, eat the things set before you. Heal the sick who are there, and tell them, "The kingdom of God has come near you." But whatever town you enter, and they don't welcome you, go out into its streets and say, "We are wiping off as a witness against you even the dust of your town that clings to our feet. Know this for certain: the kingdom of God has come near."'" Luke 10:1-11

Day 4 • The Kingdom on Your Doorstep

↕ **Read and meditate on "God's Word for Today" in the margin and spend a moment in prayer as you begin today's lesson.**

Pam's life was a wreck. She had been picked up by a truck driver headed cross-country. When he grew tired of her, he dropped her off at a truck stop in Missouri. Hungry, cold, and wasted, she landed in a caring Christian family that loved her, served her, and sacrificed for her. She periodically went to church with them and seemed to be getting her life together.

The next summer a group of youth and adults from the family's church attended Super Summer Missouri at Southwest Baptist University. When I (Richard) met Pam and asked why she had come, she told me the group had something she wanted. I asked Pam, "What if it is a person you need and not just a good life? Do you think you are ready for Him?" I sensed that God was standing on her doorstep and she didn't know it.

Life that week has hard for Pam. She didn't like the rules, she didn't like the adult class she was in, and she wanted to go home. However, when we talked about her need for Jesus and the things He had done for her, she warmed up to the idea of giving her life to Christ. But she struggled with surrendering herself to God and putting herself under His control.

Pam fumed all week, and people prayed. On Friday morning before the final chapel service, I was headed to the auditorium when I saw Pam running toward me saying, "I did it! I did it! I did it!" When the kingdom of God was on her doorstep, hell's forces did their best to block God's effort; but darkness could not overcome the light.

Just as a family reached out to Pam and met a need, the 70 in Luke 10:1-11 would reach out and change the lives of those they came in contact with.

1. **Review "God's Word for Today." Why did Jesus send out the 70?**

_____

Jesus told the 70 to find a home, respond to the hospitality, heal the sick, and tell their hosts that the kingdom of God was on their doorstep. As the

70 obeyed, they would fulfill several functions in announcing the coming of Christ's kingdom.

1. *Preparing.* They would prepare for Jesus' coming to the same place (see v. 1).
2. *Participating.* They would have the opportunity to be part of His harvest (see v. 2).
3. *Praying.* They would pray for others to be sent to God's harvest (see v. 2).
4. *Trusting.* Their obedience would test their faith in Jesus' plan (see vv. 3-5).
5. *Networking.* They would recognize and identify "a son of peace," someone who was to be part of the harvest (see v. 6).
6. *Releasing.* They would provide someone an opportunity to participate in God's harvest by releasing their resources (see vv. 7-8).
7. *Leading.* They would become a neighbor by meeting needs that others were not meeting (see v. 9).
8. *Inviting.* They would verbally declare the nearness of the kingdom of God and invite individuals to enter it (see vv. 10-12).

② **Go back and place a check mark beside any of these roles you have played in ministry.**

③ **Turn to "Kingdom-Coming Principles" on page 106 to more fully apply these principles to your ministry.**

In this passage Jesus was describing a divine encounter*—something supernatural that takes place because of God's action, not because of our doing. Just as Saul met Jesus Christ on the road to Damascus (see Acts 9:1-31), God meets people in divine encounters today. When we abide in Christ, every person we meet can result in a divine encounter.

④ **How does the previous sentence change your perspective on your daily activities?**

_____

No matter what your role is in ministering to someone—whether building a bridge, praying, meeting a need, relieving a burden, encouraging, or sharing the gospel—God is inviting the person into His kingdom through you.

⑤ **Under "My Observation Journal" in the margin, list the persons you encountered today and what you did or will do to tell them God's kingdom is near. Update "My Ministry List" on page 92 as needed.**

✳ *Divine encounter:* an opportunity God orchestrates for you to introduce someone to Jesus at a strategic moment when the person is open to receiving Him

My Observation Journal

Week 5 » Day 4

God's Word for Today

"The kingdom of heaven will be like 10 virgins who took their lamps and went out to meet the groom. Five of them were foolish and five were sensible. When the foolish took their lamps, they didn't take oil with them. But the sensible ones took oil in their flasks with their lamps. Since the groom was delayed, they all became drowsy and fell asleep. In the middle of the night there was a shout: 'Here's the groom! Come out to meet him.' Then all those virgins got up and trimmed their lamps. But the foolish ones said to the sensible ones, 'Give us some of your oil, because our lamps are going out.' The sensible ones answered, 'No, there won't be enough for us and for you. Go instead to those who sell, and buy oil for yourselves.' When they had gone to buy some, the groom arrived. Then those who were ready went in with him to the wedding banquet, and the door was shut. Later the rest of the virgins also came and said, 'Master, master, open up for us!' But he replied, 'I assure you: I do not know you!' Therefore be alert, because you don't know the day or the hour."
Matthew 25:1-13

Day 5 • The God You Can't Ignore

↕ **Read and meditate on "God's Word for Today" in the margin and spend a moment in prayer as you begin today's lesson.**

So far you have seen how ministry and service can show others the love of Christ and build a bridge to their spiritual need. You have learned how to connect with God's activity around you through five ministry actions. You have identified and worked to overcome barriers to servanthood. You have learned to assess needs and create a ministry plan to meet those needs. You have recognized the importance of drawing near to God in order to draw near to people. By now ministry to others should feel like a normal way of life for you. We hope energy and excitement about ministry are bursting like fireworks all around you!

This week concludes with a lesson about how to keep going in ministry. God provides an endless supply of power for a servant lifestyle. Your job as a minister is to stay connected to that power supply. As you become more involved in meeting others' needs, be careful not to ignore God.

I (Richard) mentioned earlier that I entered a personal relationship with Jesus Christ after I was married. About three weeks before God awoke me to the fact that I was sinner and separated from Him, my wife awakened me from a deep sleep around 2:30 a.m. one morning and said to me, "Richard, I need to be saved!" After she explained what she had been going through, we knelt beside our bed, and she said yes to the One she had been ignoring. She later told me she felt that early-morning encounter with Jesus would have been her last opportunity.

Jesus' parable in Matthew 25:1-13 illustrates the importance of being prepared when God opens a door.

1 **Review "God's Word for Today" in the margin. What did the master say to the unprepared virgins after the door was shut?**

_____

What was Jesus' warning to His listeners?

_____

People can ignore God's plan for their lives for just so long. This is true of service opportunities for believers. Don't miss out on God's best by not being ready when He shows you needs around you and calls you to meet them.

(2) **Based on what you've studied in this course, suggest things believers can do to be prepared when God calls them to minister.**

_____

_____

Circle two actions you would like to focus on in your life.

Did you mention things like abiding in Christ and practicing the Kingdom-coming principles you studied in day 4?

(3) **Read James 1:22-25 in the margin. What is required of someone who has looked into "the perfect law of freedom" (v. 25)?**

_____

What is promised for that person? _____

By receiving the gospel, you have looked into "the perfect law of freedom." Your obligation now is to keep the gospel foremost in your consciousness and continually be filled with the Spirit (see Ephesians 5:18) so that you are always ready to minister in Jesus' name and to point others to the freedom Christ offers. God promises that you will be blessed.

What do you do if you realize that you have ignored opportunities for ministry or have done things for others without having a servant spirit?
• Name what you have neglected.
• Agree with God about it: confess it as sin.
• Commit to change.
• Act on your commitment.

Use the process suggested to confess to God any ministry opportunities you have ignored. Ask Him to help you stay prepared for a lifestyle of ministry to others.

(4) Write this week's memory verses, Matthew 28:19-20, in the margin.

Don't miss out on God's best by not being ready when He shows you needs around you and calls you to meet them.

James 1:22-25
"Be doers of the word and not hearers only, deceiving yourselves. Because if anyone is a hearer of the word and not a doer, he is like a man looking at his own face in a mirror; for he looks at himself, goes away, and right away forgets what kind of man he was. But the one who looks intently into the perfect law of freedom and perseveres in it, and is not a forgetful hearer but a doer who acts—this person will be blessed in what he does."

Session 5 • Drawing Near to Christ

Opening Prayer

Learning Goals
You will—
- explain why abiding in Christ is essential to ministry;
- recognize the importance of listening to Jesus before ministering;
- define what it means to be a neighbor to someone in need;
- learn principles for announcing the coming of God's kingdom;
- identify ways to stay connected to God when ministering to others.

Reviewing Week 5
1. In pairs or triads take turns reciting your Scripture-memory verses, Matthew 28:19-20. State why you agree or disagree with this statement: "The Great Commission cannot be done at a distance; it requires you to go near the person who needs ministry" (p. 65). How did Jesus illustrate that ministry cannot be done from a distance?
2. Read John 15:1-2,5,8. Respond to activity 1 on page 66. Why is abiding in Christ essential for believers who minister to others?
3. Give examples of ways Jesus abided in a relationship with the Father.
4. Review the signs of abiding on page 67. What are areas of weakness for you? Share any commitments you made to abide in Christ (activity 4, p. 67).
5. Read Luke 10:38-42. Why did Jesus commend Mary's choice? What does sitting at Jesus' feet mean to you? What hinders you from sitting at His feet? What encourages you to sit at His feet? Why is it important to listen to Jesus as you go out to minister?
6. Share any observations from listening to Jesus (prayer activity, p. 69).
7. Discuss the examples from the Rileys' ministry on page 70. What does it mean to be a neighbor? Share ways you and your church are being neighbors to people who need to know Christ.
8. Name persons who meet the criteria of a neighbor at the top of page 71. Share any ways you ministered to these persons through the ministry actions you learned in week 1 (activity 3, p. 71).
9. Read Luke 10:1-11. Review on page 73 the roles the 70 played in announcing the coming of the Kingdom. How can you fulfill these roles as you minister?

10. Define *divine encounter* (p. 73). Describe any divine encounters you have had as you have ministered to others.
11. What ministry opportunities have you lost because you were not prepared or attentive? Identify actions you can take to make sure you are prepared when ministry opportunities arise.

Ministering to Others

1. Debrief opportunities you had this week to minister to others.
   - Did you abide in Christ and listen to Him this week?
   - How were you a neighbor to someone this week? Did you serve as a bridge builder, offer relief, intercede, show hospitality, or promote spiritual growth?
   - What happened, and what were the results?
   - How did serving the person help you connect with him or her?
   - Did you announce that God's kingdom was near?
   - Was this a divine encounter?
   - How can you pray for follow-up with these individuals?
2. Turn to "My Ministry List" on page 92 and share updates and concerns.
3. Select an individual whose salvation you are praying for and commit to minister to that person this week. Follow this process.
   - Identify one ministry activity that will meet a need, answer a question, or fulfill an interest.
   - Enlist someone to join you in ministry—a family member, a member of your Bible study or discipleship group, or someone you want to influence for Christ.
   - After ministering, debrief with the individual who joined you.
   - Record the results and plan to report at the next session.

Praying Together

Pray in pairs that God will give you a desire to draw near to Him and abide in Christ, that He will give you a willingness to draw near others to meet their needs in ministry and to point them to Him, and for the needs of persons on your ministry lists (p. 92).

Previewing Week 6

Turn to page 79 and preview the study for the coming week.

Week 6

Passing the Baton
of Service

"I will not leave you or forsake you.
Haven't I commanded you: be strong
and courageous? Do not be afraid
or discouraged, for the LORD your
God is with you wherever you go."
Joshua 1:5,9

Passing the Baton of Service

Jesus always worked to multiply His ministry so that it would continue after He was gone. He not only modeled sacrificial service to the world, but He also taught others to do the same. Eventually, He sent out His disciples to fulfill the Greatest Commandment to "love the Lord your God with all your heart, with all your soul, and with all your mind. The second is like it: Love your neighbor as yourself" (Matthew 22:37,39). This week you will learn basic principles for passing the concept of biblical servanthood to future generations of ministers.

LEARNING GOALS
This week you will—
• state why self-denial is key to sacrificial service;
• define the big picture of ministry to others;
• explain what it means to trust God's call to ministry;
• identify ways you can pass the baton of service to others.

OVERVIEW OF WEEK 6
Day 1: Denying Self to Serve
Day 2: Seeing the Big Picture
Day 3: Learning to Trust God's Call
Day 4: Becoming a Slave
Day 5: Modeling Service

VERSES TO MEMORIZE
Joshua 1:5,9

DISCIPLESHIP HELPS FOR WEEK 6
My Ministry List (p. 92)
Ideas for Ministry Actions (pp. 94–98)
Jesus' Model of Servant Leadership (p. 107)

Day 1 • Denying Self to Serve

God's Word for Today

"On the third day Abraham looked up and saw the place in the distance. Then Abraham said to his young men, 'Stay here with the donkey. The boy and I will go over there to worship; then we'll come back to you.' Abraham took the wood for the burnt offering and laid it on his son Isaac. In his hand he took the fire and the sacrificial knife, and the two of them walked on together. Then Isaac spoke to his father Abraham and said, 'My father.' And he replied, 'Here I am, my son.' Isaac said, 'The fire and the wood are here, but where is the lamb for the burnt offering?' Abraham answered, 'God Himself will provide the lamb for the burnt offering, my son.' Then the two of them walked on together. When they arrived at the place that God had told him about, Abraham built the altar there and arranged the wood. He bound his son Isaac and placed him on the altar, on top of the wood. Then Abraham reached out and took the knife to slaughter his son. But the Angel of the LORD called to him from heaven and said, 'Abraham, Abraham!'

Read and meditate on "God's Word for Today" in the margin and spend a moment in prayer as you begin today's lesson.

One night when I (David) was an interim pastor, I received a phone call to visit the local hospital for what I thought would be a celebration for the birth of a new baby boy. When I arrived, the family recalled their difficult pilgrimage over the past several years, which had included three miscarriages before finally carrying this child full term. We visited for several minutes before I prayed with the family, then left without being invited to see the child.

I thought that was odd until the next day when I visited the family again, only to find out that the child had a serious brain defect and would never live off the respirator. Unfortunately, the child died later that night. I can still recall the flood of emotions that engulfed the family, especially after they had waited so long to finally have a child.

This reminded me of Abraham's experience in Genesis 22. Abraham and Sarah had waited a lifetime before finally giving birth to Isaac (Abraham was one hundred years old). And now, as if it were some type of cruel joke, it appeared that God was going to take Isaac back as a sacrifice on a mountain in the land of Moriah.

Can you imagine the gut-wrenching, three-day pilgrimage, all the time believing you would sacrifice your child without any explanation from God? Regardless of his emotions, Abraham continued up the mountain without hesitation.

1. **Review the passage in the margin and answer these questions.**

   What did Abraham tell the men was the purpose of the journey up the mountain?

   _____

   What did Abraham say when Isaac asked about the sacrificial lamb?

   _____

When they arrived at the appointed spot, Abraham built an altar, tied up Isaac to be sacrificed, and raised his knife for the kill. Then God intervened, telling Abraham, "Do not lay a hand on the boy or do anything to him. For now I know that you fear God, since you have not withheld your only son from Me" (v. 12). As Abraham had prophesied earlier, God provided a ram for the sacrifice, and worship indeed took place.

A single theme resonates from this story: Abraham totally surrendered his life to God by denying himself. From the time God called him in verse 1, Abraham proceeded to obey God and never questioned His intentions. This total commitment to deny self and serve God is the baton Abraham passed to Isaac and future generations.

Denying self is the first requirement for becoming a sacrificial servant.

② **Can you honestly say that the baton of service you are passing along is one of self-denial and total commitment to God?**   ○ Yes ○ No

Self-sacrifice defined the heart of Christ, just as it defined the ministry of Abraham.

③ **Read Mark 8:34-35 in the margin. Underline each action required to follow Jesus.**
What does it look like for you to deny yourself? _____
_____

How is it possible for you to save your life by first losing it? _____
_____

What does taking up your cross represent in your life? _____
_____

④ **Invite up to three persons you know to join you in an act of service to an unsaved neighbor, coworker, or acquaintance. Examine "Ideas for Ministry Actions" on pages 94–98. How will you minister?**
_____

⑤ **Start memorizing your memory verses for this week, Joshua 1:5,9. If you would like, tear out and use the card at the back of the book.**

He replied, 'Here I am.' Then He said, 'Do not lay a hand on the boy or do anything to him. For now I know that you fear God, since you have not withheld your only son from Me.' Abraham looked up and saw a ram caught by its horns in the thicket. So Abraham went and took the ram and offered it as a burnt offering in place of his son." Genesis 22:4-14

Mark 8:34-35
"If anyone wants to be My follower, he must deny himself, take up his cross, and follow Me. For whoever wants to save his life will lose it, but whoever loses his life because of Me and the gospel will save it."

Watch and Pray
Spend time in prayer surrendering your desires to God. If you are ready, tell God that your answer is always yes, no matter where or whom He calls you to serve in the future.

God's Word for Today

"After the death of Moses the LORD's servant, the LORD spoke to Joshua son of Nun, who had served Moses: 'Moses My servant is dead. Now you and all the people prepare to cross over the Jordan to the land I am giving the Israelites. I have given you every place where the sole of your foot treads, just as I promised Moses. Your territory will be from the wilderness and Lebanon to the great Euphrates River—all the land of the Hittites—and west to the Mediterranean Sea. No one will be able to stand against you as long as you live. I will be with you, just as I was with Moses. I will not leave you or forsake you. Be strong and courageous, for you will distribute the land I swore to their fathers to give them as an inheritance. Above all, be strong and very courageous to carefully observe the whole instruction My servant Moses commanded you. Do not turn from it to the right or the left, so that you will have success wherever you go. This book of instruction must not depart from your mouth; you are to recite it day and night,

Day 2 • Seeing the Big Picture

Read and meditate on "God's Word for Today" in the margin and spend a moment in prayer as you begin today's lesson.

A friend recently e-mailed me (David) the following story. A holy man was having a conversation with the Lord one day and said, "Lord, I would like to know what heaven and hell are like." The Lord led the holy man to two doors. He opened one of the doors, and the holy man looked in. In the middle of the room was a large, round table. In the middle of the table was a large pot of stew, which smelled delicious and made the holy man's mouth water. The people sitting around the table were thin and sickly and appeared to be famished. They were holding spoons with very long handles that were strapped to their arms, and each was able to reach into the pot of stew and take a spoonful. But because the handle was longer than their arms, they could not get the spoons back into their mouths. The holy man shuddered at the sight of their misery and suffering. The Lord said, "You have seen hell."

They went to the next room and opened the door. It was exactly the same as the first one. There was the large, round table with the large pot of stew that made the holy man's mouth water. The people were equipped with the same long-handled spoons, but here the people were well nourished and plump, laughing and talking. The holy man said, "I don't understand."

"It is simple," said the Lord. "It requires but one skill. You see, they have learned to feed one another, while the greedy think only of themselves."

This is what is meant by seeing the big picture. Joshua 1 reveals that Moses had obviously mentored and prepared Joshua for the time when he would pass away. He did not see Joshua as a rival to be shunned for selfish fear that he would steal the limelight. On the contrary, Joshua was a companion in ministry. Moses had prepared him to serve both God and others.

If Moses had not been willing to prepare Joshua for the ultimate responsibility of leading several million Israelites into the promised land after his death, they may well have ended up like the thin and sickly people who could not see beyond their own selfish needs.

1. Your memory verses for this week convey the essence of God's words to Joshua. Write them here.

_____

_____

What did Joshua do in response?

_____

Even though Joshua was grief-stricken by the death of his mentor and overwhelmed by the challenge, he responded in the manner in which he had been prepared. He simply commanded the officers to "go through the camp and tell the people, 'Get provisions ready for yourselves, for within three days you will be crossing the Jordan to go in and take possession of the land the LORD your God is giving you to inherit.'" Moses had trained Joshua to keep the big picture in mind—the ministry God had for him.

Seeing the big picture is essential to becoming an effective servant. This principle requires the ability to see beyond your selfish desires and beyond the obstacles to capture God's vision of service for Him and others.

2. How would you define the big picture of ministry to others?

_____

3. Can you look beyond your desires to see others' needs? ○ Yes ○ No
Can you look beyond momentary challenges to see how God
can use you to manifest His love to a hurting world? ○ Yes ○ No
Can you swallow your pride and ignore self-recognition
to become a "Moses" to someone in your life? ○ Yes ○ No

Take a few minutes to pray and ask God to reveal the persons He wants you to mentor, helping them become ministers to others. Record the names of your "Joshuas" in the margin.

4. Invite your "Joshuas" to go with you to serve someone. Suggestions include visiting seniors, volunteering at a food bank, teaching English as a second language, reading stories to children, and tutoring. Also examine "Ideas for Ministry Actions" on pages 94–98. Serve Christ and others while encouraging your "Joshuas" to develop a lifestyle of servanthood. Then update "My Ministry List," page 92.

so that you may carefully observe everything written in it. For then you will prosper and succeed in whatever you do. Haven't I commanded you: be strong and courageous? Do not be afraid or discouraged, for the LORD your God is with you wherever you go.' Then Joshua commanded the officers of the people: 'Go through the camp and tell the people, "Get provisions ready for yourselves, for within three days you will be crossing the Jordan to go in and take possession of the land the LORD your God is giving you to inherit."'" Joshua 1:1-11

My "Joshuas"

Watch and Pray
Pray that God will help you see beyond your own desires to recognize the needs of others and to mentor someone to be a minister.

Day 3 • Learning to Trust God's Call

"Look, I'm sending you out like sheep among wolves. Therefore be as shrewd as serpents and as harmless as doves. Because people will hand you over to sanhedrins and flog you in their synagogues, beware of them. You will even be brought before governors and kings because of Me, to bear witness to them and to the nations. But when they hand you over, don't worry about how or what you should speak. For you will be given what to say at that hour, because you are not speaking, but the Spirit of your Father is speaking through you. You will be hated by everyone because of My name. But the one who endures to the end will be delivered." Matthew 10:16-20,22

Read and meditate on "God's Word for Today" in the margin and spend a moment in prayer as you begin today's lesson.

Several years ago I (David) visited an elderly man in the hospital who was not expected to live more than a few days. As we discussed points from my recent sermon series on the Book of Hebrews, the man uncharacteristically began to cry. At first I thought I might have said something that prompted his emotional outburst. However, I soon realized that his response had nothing to do with our conversation. With a broken voice he simply stated, "I cannot die now and go before God empty-handed."

I was confused. The man appeared to be a model Christian, having received Christ as a boy. When I asked him to explain further, he confessed that he had never shared his faith, even though he could recall countless neighbors, friends, and family members who desperately needed Christ.

I could not believe my ears. Here was a wealthy man lying on his deathbed; yet his final and greatest concern was a broken heart over his disobedience to love and serve others enough to share Christ with them. At this point his only fear was that he would die without being able to fulfill God's call. He felt as if he had wasted his life on frivolous pursuits.

I knelt beside the bed and asked God to grant the man's request for more time to complete the task of serving and sharing with the hurting people in his sphere of influence. God granted that request. Contrary to the doctor's prediction, the man was back at home three days later.

With a renewed vision he was a totally different man until his death a year later. At his funeral I was reassured that he had confronted his secret sin. Just before I stood to share the funeral sermon, his teenage grandson read several Bible verses and led in prayer. Little did the grandson know that his name had been the first mentioned by a brokenhearted grandfather a year earlier. Praise the Lord, he was now a Christian!

The principle of trusting God's call is essential to becoming an effective servant of God and others. Unfortunately, most Christians are like the elderly man. We spend a lifetime living a religious but selfish existence with little regard for the souls of people around us. We are afraid to do what Jesus called His disciples to do.

We spend a lifetime living a religious but selfish existence with little regard for the souls of people around us.

1. **Review "God's Word for Today" and answer these questions.**
   Why would the disciples need to trust God as they went out to serve?

   _____

   How would they know what to say to the authorities? _____

   _____

Jesus has given you the call. He has given you the good news. He has given you His Spirit. What's holding you back?

2. **Identify any fears that keep you from trusting God's call to go and serve others in His name and to train others to serve.**

   _____

The number one reason Christians shy away from trusting God and serving others is fear of rejection. But is it rational to automatically assume that people will not appreciate someone who voluntarily meets a need in their lives and shares the greatest news ever heard? It's time to trust God's call.

Proverbs 3:5-6

"Trust in the LORD with all your heart, and do not rely on your own understanding; think about Him in all your ways, and He will guide you on the right paths."

3. **Read Proverbs 3:5-6 in the margin. What would your service look like if you trusted God this way?**

   _____

   _____

Nell Kerley was a well-respected 66-year-old Sunday School teacher who began sharing her faith while taking *FAITH Evangelism*. Now 75 and in poor health, Nell has brought more than 2,500 people to Christ. Nell says her Christian life was incomplete until she learned to fully trust God's call to serve others and share the gospel. She mentors others to do the same.

Watch and Pray
Pray for God to help you learn to trust His call and serve others without reservation. Ask Him to open your heart and life to the needs of hurting people in your workplace, family, and neighborhood.

4. Take a friend or a family member with you to meet a need. Model how to pray for others, mow someone's grass, take a meal to a fire station, wash a neighbor's car, or deliver cookies. Also examine the activities in "Ideas for Ministry Actions" on pages 94–98. After ministering, update "My Ministry List" on page 92.

Day 4 • Becoming a Slave

Read and meditate on "God's Word for Today" in the margin and spend a moment in prayer as you begin today's lesson.

A pastor friend was concluding a series of messages aimed at mobilizing his rural congregation into the harvest fields of southeastern Ohio. In keeping with his passion, he taught the basic principles of servant evangelism, ending with a challenge for the congregation to surrender everything to Christ and to ask Him what they could do for the benefit of His kingdom.

An elderly church member desperately wanted to make a difference. Being a person of very modest means, she went to a discount store to purchase something she could give to her neighbors. She pondered, *What is something everyone uses and needs?*

The only necessity the woman could afford was several packages of toilet paper. So, yes, she actually went door to door in her small community and passed out toilet paper, explaining that her pastor had challenged her to give away something that might help her get to know her neighbors because she loved Jesus and wanted everyone else to love Him too! She later delivered freshly baked cookies to the most receptive neighbors.

I (David) am not advocating a toilet-paper ministry; but as we conclude this study about what it means to be a servant, I have to wonder what would happen if every believer caught the same spirit as this sweet lady. This is a perfect example of how a person can be challenged and mentored to surrender everything to become a servant and impact the world for Christ. She reminds me of a certain woman in Scripture.

1. Read Mark 12:41-44 in the margin on page 87. Why did Jesus commend the woman's action?

_____

_____

This woman willingly gave all she had out of radical love for her Lord. What about you? Maybe you've been ministering throughout this course, but now it's time to serve in another way—by sacrificially giving your time and resources to mentor another person for service in the Kingdom. Maybe God wants you to move to a new level of servanthood.

Consider the example of Christ, our perfect model of servant ministry.

(2) **Review "God's Word for Today" on the previous page. Underline words Paul used to illustrate Jesus' servant nature.**

Based on Jesus' example, what should our servant ministry look like?

_____

_____

A seminary professor gave each student five dollars to use in an act of service that would create a conversation about Christ. He instructed the students to serve with no strings attached; to simply show kindness; and if the person asked why, to share a brief testimony. Some of the students went to restaurants and cleaned toilets, while others purchased donuts for businesses and teacher's lounges in schools. Some went to public laundries and paid to wash several loads of clothes for patrons.

One student wanted to model radical servanthood for his four sons. Armed with plastic gloves and small trash bags, he and his sons walked through their neighborhood and cleaned up yards for neighbors who had dogs. As you might imagine, this act of humble service created many discussions. After several months of modeling, this father was able to pass the greatest baton to his sons by leading one of the neighbors to Christ.

(3) **Complete "Jesus' Model of Servant Leadership" on page 107. How are you modeling servant ministry for the person(s) to whom you are passing the baton of service?**

_____

_____

What do you need to empty yourself of and submit to God in order to reflect a servant heart to those you serve and those you mentor?

_____

(4) **Practicing saying aloud your memory verses, Joshua 1:5,9. Encourage the person(s) you are mentoring by sharing the verses with them.**

Mark 12:41-44

"Sitting across from the temple treasury, He [Jesus] watched how the crowd dropped money into the treasury. Many rich people were putting in large sums. And a poor widow came and dropped in two tiny coins worth very little. Summoning His disciples, He said to them, 'I assure you: This poor widow has put in more than all those giving to the temple treasury. For they all gave out of their surplus, but she out of her poverty has put in everything she possessed—all she had to live on.' "

↑↓ **Watch and Pray**
Pray through Philippians 2:3-11 and surrender to God as His sacrificial servant.

Day 5 • Modeling Service

God's Word for Today

"James and John, the sons of Zebedee, approached Him and said, 'Teacher, we want You to do something for us if we ask You?' 'What do you want me to do for you?' He asked them. They answered Him, 'Allow us to sit at Your right and Your left in Your glory.' But Jesus said to them, 'You don't know what you're asking. Are you able to drink the cup I drink or be baptized with the baptism I am being baptized with?' 'We are able,' they told Him. Jesus called them over and said to them, 'You know that those who are regarded as rulers of the Gentiles dominate them, and their men of high positions exercise power over them. But it must not be like that among you. On the contrary, whoever wants to be great among you must be your servant, and whoever wants to be first among you must be a slave to all. For even the Son of Man did not come to be served, but to serve, and to give His life— a ransom for many.' "
Mark 10:35-39,42-45

My (David's) dad was a master at passing the baton of service. I will never forget the lesson he taught me at Christmas in 1968. Because my mom had been very ill with a kidney disease, my dad was working an extra job at Western Auto to try to pay medical debts. It was Christmas Eve, and I was in the store when Dad called me to the back room and told me to load our car with a large stack of toys he had purchased from the showroom.

I was wondering about the toys as I rode with Dad toward home. When we pulled into our subdivision, Dad took a different route and drove to a house on the street behind ours. I will never forget the look on our neighbor's face when Dad went to the door and informed this newly divorced mother, who had no hope of securing toys for her three kids, that God hears our prayers.

I had more fun unloading those toys than I did opening mine the next morning. I can't remember what I received that Christmas, but I will never forget what we gave. That "baton" has stuck with me.

Dad viewed things differently than most people did. Who else would grow six hundred tomato plants? When the tomatoes began to come in, Dad went to every ballpark and public arena and gave them away as an opportunity for ministry. He also delivered boxes of tomatoes to local vegetable stands at no charge just so that he could share Christ's love.

The baton of service was the greatest gift my father gave me. His life modeled humility, compassion, and love. And he was willing to sacrifice because he loved God and people more than himself. When he died, hundreds of people lined up for more than nine hours to share how he provided groceries and paid electric bills. I preached my father's funeral. In closing, I held up a track baton, equated it to my father's servant legacy, then laid it on his casket with the final question "Who will pick it up?"

1. **Identify someone who passed the baton of service to you.**

_____

How did they demonstrate Christlike service to others?

_____

Mark 10:35-39,42-45 illustrates the attitude Christ wants His children to have toward a hurting world.

2) **Review "God's Word for Today" and check the statement that best describes your attitude.**
○ Like James and John, I feel entitled to ask Jesus for a seat of honor.
○ Unlike James and John, I am ready to be a servant to others.

Jesus reminds us, "Whoever wants to be great among you must be your servant, and whoever wants to be first among you must be a slave to all. For even the Son of Man did not come to be served, but to serve, and to give His life—a ransom for many" (Mark 10:43-45).

3) **If you died today, what would your friends and family say about your legacy of service to others?**

_____

_____

Jerry Pipes has reported that "88 percent of those who grow up in our evangelical churches leave at age 18 and do not come back."[1] Think of the implications. Churches spend millions of dollars each year on youth ministries but graduate only a little more than 10 percent from high school as devoted followers of Christ and His church. However, the percentage of high-school graduates who leave church falls from 88 percent to less than 4 percent when youth serve others alongside their parents.[2] If you want to make a lasting difference with your family, pass the baton of service.

4) **What are you doing to involve your children in service to others?**

_____

If you don't have children, continue investing your life in the "Joshuas" you identified in day 2.

Because Christ lives in you, servanthood is not an activity but part of your spiritual DNA. Go impact your community for Christ by praying, serving, loving, and sharing.

5) **Examine "Ideas for Ministry Actions" on pages 94–98 and ask God to show you where He wants you to be involved.**

> Because Christ lives in you, servanthood is not an activity but part of your spiritual DNA.

Watch and Pray
Examine your legacy of service. Ask God to teach you how to pass the baton of service to your children or to others in your life.

1. Victor Lee and Jerry Pipes, *Family to Family* (Alpharetta, GA: The North American Mission Board of the Southern Baptist Convention, 1999), 1.
2. *Family to Family* video.

Session 6 • Passing the Baton of Service

Opening Prayer

Learning Goals
You will—
- state why self-denial is key to sacrificial service;
- define the big picture of ministry to others;
- explain what it means to trust God's call to ministry;
- identify ways you can pass the baton of service to others.

Reviewing Week 6

1. In pairs or triads take turns reciting your Scripture-memory verses, Joshua 1:5,9. Identify resources God provides for your ministry to others.

2. Summarize the account in Genesis 22:4-14. How did Abraham demonstrate self-denial?

3. Read Mark 8:34-35. Answer the questions in activity 3 on page 81. Are you completely surrendered to God's service? What areas do you struggle with?

4. Share experiences ministering to an unsaved neighbor, coworker, or acquaintance (activity 4, p. 81).

5. Read Joshua 1:1-11. Who prepared Joshua for service? What was God's promise to Joshua? What was the big picture for Joshua? What does it mean to keep your eyes on the big picture as you minister to others? What obstacles make it hard to see ways God can use you?

6. Name the "Joshuas" to whom you are passing the baton of service. Share experiences ministering with them this week (activity 4, p. 83).

7. Read Matthew 10:16-20,22. How did the disciples know what to say when they were taken before the authorities? Can witnesses rely on the same help today?

8. Express agreement or disagreement with this statement from day 3: "We spend a lifetime living a religious but selfish existence with little regard for the souls of people around us" (p. 85). Are you trusting God's call to ministry or shrinking back? If you are hesitating, why? Read Proverbs 3:5-6.

9. Share ministry experiences from activity 4, page 85.

10. Read Philippians 2:3-11. How did Jesus demonstrate servanthood?
11. Review "Jesus' Model of Servant Leadership" on page 107. Answer the questions in activity 3 on page 87.
12. If your final epitaph were written today, what would it say? Take three minutes and write some key ideas.
13. Evaluate your epitaph with your group members. Would you have a legacy of service, sacrifice, and changed lives?
14. Read Mark 10:43b-45. Review the principles for passing the baton of service that you studied this week. As a parent, friend, or mentor, how will you pass the baton of service to others? To whom will you pass it?

Ministering to Others

1. Consider these ideas for modeling service to others.
   - Take your children into your community to meet needs. Rake leaves, shovel snow, mow yards, pull weeds, or deliver cookies.
   - Invite a friend to join you to serve at a food pantry, volunteer at a hospital, or feed local firefighters.
   - Ask your pastor to assign an interested church member for you to mentor as a servant. Take the person with you to clean toilets at local restaurants, provide umbrella escorts on rainy days, or paint or repair someone's house.
2. Would you want to lead a group study of *Growing Disciples: Minister to Others* as a way to pass the baton?
3. Examine "Ideas for Ministry Actions" on pages 94–98 and discuss future ministry possibilities.
4. Examine "My Ministry List" on page 92. How have you involved others in service this week? Who needs to be added to the list?

Praying Together

1. Spend time in individual prayer about being a minister to others and about mentoring others to be servants.
2. Close by praying as a group for each participant's role in ministry, for servants to be mentored, and for persons you know who need caring ministry. Pray that God will create a servant movement through His children and that He will be glorified as a result.

My Ministry List

Keep a running list of ministry contacts as directed in the lessons of this study. Make additional copies as needed. Also consider making copies of this page to keep a list of ministry contacts after this study is over. Try to add at least one individual to the list each month. That means at the end of one year, you will have focused God's resources on 12 individuals. When someone is saved, adjust your ministry to become a personal trainer (see week 1, day 5).

Name	Relationship	Ministry Action/ Date	Witness/Date	Response

Profile of a Servant Lifestyle

Use the following profile to identify individuals who model ministry to others by writing their names in the blanks beside the qualities that apply to them. Then assess your own servant lifestyle by checking the qualities you exhibit. Look for areas in which God wants to manifest Himself in and through your life.

Someone You
Observed   You

_____ ◯ 1. A servant gives evidence of possessing new life in Christ (see 2 Corinthians 5:17).

_____ ◯ 2. A servant's attitude toward sin and sinners is like that of Jesus (see Luke 5:32).

_____ ◯ 3. A servant gives evidence of a Christlike attitude toward self (see Philippians 2:5-8).

_____ ◯ 4. A servant recognizes God's activity around him and joins God in what He is doing.

_____ ◯ 5. By serving others, a servant is increasingly effective at building relational bridges through which he intentionally shares the gospel.

_____ ◯ 6. A servant is openly identified with Jesus Christ where she lives and works, manifests a heart for witnessing to what she knows to be true about Jesus Christ, clearly and appropriately gives her personal testimony, and regularly presents the gospel with increasing effectiveness (see Matthew 5:16; Colossians 4:6; 1 Peter 3:15).

_____ ◯ 7. As a learner, a servant is open and teachable (see Acts 17:11).

              ◯ 8. As a leader, a servant leads others to join him in meeting needs and telling the good news of Jesus Christ (see Mark 1:38; 2 Timothy 2:2).

What steps does God want you to take to allow Him to work more effectively in and through you? Ask Him. _____

_____

_____

_____

Ideas for Ministry Actions

Consider serving others in Jesus' name through the following actions. Be prepared to provide all services free, no donations accepted, no strings attached.

In the "Equipment" column, you will frequently see references to cards. Whether service is done when the person is present or away, you will need to prepare cards to leave behind that identify and remind the individual of the source of the ministry action. Create cards that resemble business cards. On one side include the name of the church with directions and a place for the persons who serve to write their names. On the other side use words like "An act of kindness with no strings attached" and a Scripture verse like John 3:16.

PROJECT	CONCEPT	EQUIPMENT	COST	WEATHER
Single moms' oil change	Meet a need of single moms, who regularly have car problems.	Cards, filters, oil	Cost of oil and filters	Any except extreme cold
Windshield washing	Wash windshields in driveways, at gas pumps, or outside stores.	Cards, squeegees, squirt bottles, cleaner, rags	Minimal	Clear and moderate. If it's too hot, the fluid will evaporate.
Mother's Day carnation giveaway	Set up outside grocery store on Saturday before Mother's Day.	Cards, table, sign, flowers	Minimal	Any
Sunday-morning newspaper and coffee giveaway	Go door to door early in the morning to houses without newspapers in front.	Cards, Sunday newspapers, coffee	Price of newspapers in bulk	Dry
Snow removal	Help people dig out of snow.	Cards, shovels, coffee	Minimal	Snow
Pulling out cars stuck in snow	Rescue people from ditches or otherwise stranded.	Cards, shovels, chains, bag of grit or salt pellets, coffee	Minimal	Snow
Returning empty garbage cans from street	Bring cans back to peoples' houses.	Cards	None	Any

Food for shut-ins	Deliver food to shut-ins.	Cards	None	Any
Outdoor window washing	Offer to wash first-floor windows.	Cards, professional squeegees, cleaner, short ladder, buckets	Minimal	Dry
Yard cleanup or lawn care	Clean up messy yards or do mowing and trimming.	Cards, bags, rakes, mower	Gasoline, oil, and trash bags	Dry
Easter-basket giveaway	Give Easter baskets to children.	Cards, baskets, candy, Christian literature or tapes	Cost of baskets	Any
Rainy-day grocery escort	Help shoppers to cars with packages.	Cards, golf umbrellas	Minimal	Rainy
Home repair	Offer repairs within your capabilities.	Cards, basic tool kit	Limit work to your capable-repair budget.	Dry if working outdoors
House/apartment/dorm cleaning	Offer to clean. May need to call ahead or work from referrals.	Cards, vacuum cleaners, brooms, trash bags	Minimal	Any
Winter car wash	Spray off underside grime of cars.	Cards, coffee, wands	Minimal	Below 20 degrees, door locks could freeze.
Summer car wash	Use banners that say, "Free Car Wash— No Kidding"	Cards, basic wash equipment, banners. Can also serve drinks and play music.	Minimal. Use a sports bar's parking lot and pay for the water.	Dry, above 60 degrees
Filling windshield-washer fluid	Refill washer reserves in cars and clean off wiper blades.	Cards, washer fluid, signs, table	Cost of fluid	Dry
Checking air in tires	Check whether tires are properly inflated and adjust pressure if necessary.	Cards, compressor or portable air bubbles, air-pressure gauges	Minimal for pressure gauges. Borrow compressors or air tanks.	Any, but there is greater concern in summer.

Memorial services	Provide complimentary memorial services for families of deceased who had no church affiliation.	Cards	Advertising in newspaper or telephone book	Any
Carbon-monoxide detectors	Give out complimentary carbon-monoxide detectors. Return in a few days.	Cards, detectors	Cost of detectors in bulk	Usually winter
Smoke-detector batteries	Give out complimentary smoke-detector batteries.	Cards, reminders with date, batteries	Cost of batteries in bulk	Any
Lightbulb service	Go door to door and offer to changed burned-out bulbs.	Cards, 15- to 60-watt bulbs, stepladder	Cost of lightbulbs in bulk	Any
Self-service laundry outreach	Pay for washing and drying clothes at self-service laundries.	Cards, rolls of quarters	Cost of washing and drying	Any
Blood-pressure screening	Check blood pressure in public places.	Cards, stethoscopes, sphygmomanometers	Initial investment necessary. Many nurses have equipment.	Any
Checking car safety lights	Replace burned-out bulbs in cars.	Cards, variety of spare bulbs, screwdrivers	Replacement bulbs vary in price.	Dry
Killing weeds	Spray for weeds on sidewalks and in driveways.	Cards, weed killer, sprayers, gloves, masks	Weed killer varies in price. The least expensive is to buy in gallons and dilute in sprayers.	Warm, dry, usually summer
Sealing cracks in blacktop driveways	Patch homeowners' driveways. Use flyers to get interest.	Cards, sealer, sealer brooms	Varies—check with hardware stores for prices of one- to five-gallon cans.	Warm, dry

Cleaning house gutters	Clean leaves, sticks, and debris from house gutters.	Cards, gloves, ladders, trash bags	Minimal. Everyone can bring his own ladder.	Dry
Organizing birthday parties	Organize and run parties for children. Advertise in local newspapers.	Cards, activities, favors, music	Parents pay for supplies. Use ads in free and local papers.	Dry and warm if outdoors
Food collection for the poor or for a food bank	Distribute flyers door to door. Return a week later to pick up cans and dry goods.	Cards, bags	Minimal	Any
Vacuuming car interiors	Set up in a mall parking lot or gas station to vacuum cars.	Cards, canister vacuums, hand-held vacuums	Minimal. Volunteers can bring their vacuum cleaners.	Dry
Raking leaves	Offer to rake leaves.	Cards, rakes, bags, blowers	Rakes and bags	Dry, usually autumn
Wrapping Christmas gifts	Build a simple booth and set up at the mall.	Cards, paper, ribbons, tape, scissors.	Cost of paper, ribbons, and tape	Any
Soft-drink or frozen-treat giveaway	Set up tables at store exits or sporting events.	Cards, drinks or treats, ice chests, ice, table, sign	Lower cost by buying in quantity.	Warm or hot
Coffee giveaway	Set up tables at store exits, sporting events or a bus stop and serve hot coffee.	Cards, table, coffee, creamers, sugar, stirrers, dispensers, sign	Minimal	Cool or cold
Packing bags at grocery stores	Go to a self-bagging grocery store and help people bag their groceries.	Cards; button that reads, "Just because"	No cost	Any
Balloon giveaway	Go to a park and give balloons and cards to children with parents.	Cards, helium tanks, balloons	Cost of balloons and helium	Any
Bird feeders	Provide free bird feeders and refills to convalescent centers.	Cards, bird feeders, birdseed	Birdseed, initial investment in feeders	Any

Painting house numbers on curbs	Offer to paint address numbers on the curb.	Cards, stencils, spray paint	Minimal	Dry, warm
Community dinner	Throw a party for a neighborhood.	Cards, food choice	Cost depends on type of meal.	Any
Shopping assistance	Shop for shut-ins.	Cards, vehicles	Minimal	Any
Christmas-tree removal	Collect and dispose of trees after Christmas.	Cards	None	Any
Shoe-shining service	Offer free shoe shining at stores, malls, and other public places.	Cards, shoe polish, rags, kits	Minimal	Any unless outdoors

Adapted from Steven Sjogren, *Conspiracy of Kindness*, as used in *Servanthood Evangelism Manual* (Alpharetta, GA: The North American Mission Board of the Southern Baptist Convention, 1999). Used by permission.

For other creative ideas and helps, see *Ministry Evangelism Tool Kit* (Alpharetta, GA: The North American Mission Board of the Southern Baptist Convention). To order, call (866) 407-6262 or visit *www.namb.net/ministry* or *www.servantevangelism.com*.

Ministry Action Plan

Person to whom you will minister:

_____

As you follow the SERVE process to plan your ministry, follow the directions to record the requested information after each step.

S *Search* your heart and check your motives through intimate prayer. Nothing significant ever occurs for God without prayer. Ask God to give you sensitivity to the needs of others.

Stop and pray for this person.

E *Evaluate* the needs around you by opening your heart and your eyes. Slow down and allow yourself to see and experience the needs. Ask God to give you wisdom and a plan to meet the needs.

What is the person's ministry need?

_____

How does God want you to help meet this need? List each action step.

_____

_____

When will you begin the ministry?

_____

R *Resource* the need by considering funds, food, equipment, and so on. Be generous and open to ways God may lead you to meet the needs of others. It doesn't require wealth but faithfulness.

What resources do you need to minister to this person?

_____

_____

Does anyone else need to be involved or informed? If so, who?

_____

What difficulties do you anticipate?

_____

V *Vacate* your comfort zone and put your plan into action. Don't just talk about the need. Go meet it!

How did the person respond to your ministry?

_____

Did you have an opportunity to share the gospel? If so, what was the person's response?

_____

What additional ministry steps do you need to take with this person?

_____

E *Evaluate* the response to improve future ministry. If something works, how can you improve it? If it fails, ask why; then don't repeat it.

What worked well when you ministered?

_____

How can you improve your ministry next time?

_____

Community Prayerwalking

Prayer is one of the most effective ways you can minister to others because it connects human needs with God's power and provision. Prayerwalking in your community is a great way to combine prayer and witness in a natural, nonintrusive way. T. W. Hunt has written, "Prayerwalking is simply what it says—praying while you walk. It is praying with open eyes and an open heart while walking through a particular area, asking God to do a special work in that place. … When you pray onsite, God seems to bring people and needs more sharply into focus."[1]

Prayerwalking draws believers closer to God and gives them a vision for the lost. This focused prayer releases God's power and love as believers agree with His plans for an area. Prayerwalking also helps each believer focus on his or her responsibility to reach the neighborhood. Prayerwalking can help believers saturate the community with prayer in preparation for ministry, witnessing, community surveys, or other outreach.

You can prayerwalk alone, but Jesus promised His presence and power when two or more pray together (see Matthew 18:19-20). Sometimes it is also safer to prayerwalk with others. Have a cell phone with you if possible.

For direct contact with the area you want God to touch, travel to that community. Walk and pray with your head up and your eyes open. Your goals are to cover the area with prayer and to listen for the Holy Spirit to speak to you, based on what you see, hear, and smell.

You don't need to stop in front of a home or a business. As you walk by, silently or softly pray a prayer based on what you sense from the Spirit. Prayers should be short and specific. For example, you might pray for—
• physical, material, and spiritual needs;
• transformation of the neighborhood;
• preparation for ministry or witnessing;
• receptivity to the gospel;
• salvation;
• strengthening of churches and families.

As you walk and pray, observe the following. You may want to make notes.
• Good or harmful influences
• Needs that you or your church could meet
• Churches, ministries, organizations, and agencies that already exist

Be sensitive and responsive to a divine encounter—an opportunity when the Spirit leads someone into the path of a believer so that they can hear the gospel, be encouraged, or receive ministry.

Report the results of your experience to your group or church.

Adapted from *Community Assessment Manual*, *www.namb.net*, 8–9.

1. T. W. Hunt, *The Life-Changing Power of Prayer* (Nashville: LifeWay Press, 2002), 86.

Equipped to SERVE

God has uniquely prepared you to serve by equipping you in five key areas. Those areas can be identified by the acrostic SERVE.

S   *Spiritual gifts*—gifts God gives through His Spirit to empower you for service

E   *Experiences*—events God allows in your life that mold you into a servant leader

R   *Relational style*—behavioral traits God uses to give you a leadership style

V   *Vocational skills*—abilities you have gained through training and experience that you can use in service to God

E   *Enthusiasm*—passion God has put in your heart for a particular ministry

By identifying your spiritual gifts, experiences, relational style, vocational skills, and enthusiasm, you can understand how God has equipped you for servant ministry.

SPIRITUAL GIFTS

A spiritual gift is "a manifestation of the Spirit" (1 Corinthians 12:7). It is not a special ability you develop on your own; that is a skill or a talent. You do not seek a spiritual gift. Instead, you prayerfully seek to understand how God will demonstrate Himself through you for His purposes.

God gives spiritual gifts for the common good of the church, to equip and build up the body of Christ. Spiritual gifts are not for pride but for service. Your goal as a servant is to discover how God in His grace has gifted you for service.

Romans 12:6-8; 1 Corinthians 12:8-10,28-30; Ephesians 4:11; and 1 Peter 4:9-11 contain representative lists of gifts God has given to the church:[1]

- Leadership (see Romans 12:8)
- Administration (see 1 Corinthians 12:28)
- Teaching (see Romans 12:7; 1 Corinthians 12:28; Ephesians 4:11)
- Knowledge (see 1 Corinthians 12:8)
- Wisdom (see 1 Corinthians 12:8)
- Prophecy (see Romans 12:6; 1 Corinthians 12:10)
- Discernment (see 1 Corinthians 12:10)
- Exhortation (see Romans 12:8)
- Shepherding (see Ephesians 4:11)
- Faith (see 1 Corinthians 12:9)
- Evangelism (see Ephesians 4:11)
- Apostleship (see 1 Corinthians 12:28; Ephesians 4:11)
- Service/helps (see Romans 12:7; 1 Corinthians 12:28)
- Mercy (see Romans 12:8)
- Giving (see Romans 12:8)
- Hospitality (see 1 Peter 4:9)

A spiritual-gifts inventory and scoring instrument can be found at *www.lifeway.com*.

EXPERIENCES

Servants of Christ trust that God works in their personal histories to bring about His plans for their lives. Experiences are God's crucible to mold you into His image. God can use what has already happened in your life to accomplish His will. He can mold you into a tool of His grace. He can break into your life and use you for His purposes, as He did with Paul (see Acts 22:3-21).

Henry Blackaby calls these events spiritual markers. A spiritual marker "identifies a time of transition, decision, or direction when I clearly know that God has guided me."[2] Spiritual markers remind you that God is at work in your history. Remembering them helps you see God's work in your life and how He is unfolding His plan for you.

You have events when God made His will clear to you. God broke into history, and you know God spoke to you. He may have confirmed a decision you had made. He may have revealed something new about who He is. Don't worry if you do not have a dramatic story. God works in everyday events to shape you into His likeness.

God is at work around you and always has been. He can use any event in your life to guide you to His kingdom purposes.

RELATIONAL STYLE

How you relate to others is basic to know how you serve. To know your relational style is to know how God has molded you to serve people through your relationships with them.

God will help you understand your role as a servant as you assess the strengths and weaknesses of your relational style. A proven relational survey can be found in Ken Voges's workbook *Understanding How Others*

Misunderstand You. Voges uses the letters DISC to represent four primary relational styles:

D *Dominant style*—works toward achieving goals and results; functions best in active, challenging environments

I *Influencing style*—works toward relating to people through verbal persuasion; functions best in friendly, favorable environments

S *Steadiness style*—works toward supporting and cooperating with others; functions best in supportive, harmonious environments

C *Conscientious style*—works toward doing things right and focuses best on details; functions best in structured, orderly environments[3]

The DISC survey is included in the workbook *Jesus on Leadership*. Other relational profiles are offered by Ministry Insights, *www.ministryinsights.com*, and Tim LaHaye, *Spirit-Controlled Temperament*. Completing a survey will reveal your relational strengths and how you can use them to minister.

VOCATIONAL SKILLS

Our English word *vocation* comes from the Latin word *vocare*, meaning *to call*. A vocation, then, is what you feel called to do with your life. A sense of divine calling was once part of a person's place in the world. A vocation was part of God's plan for a person's life. God called, and you responded by gaining the skills necessary to live out that calling. In today's secular world, *vocation* means any profession or occupation. A vocational skill is any ability you have learned that enhances your calling in life.

Paul encouraged the Christians in Ephesus to "walk worthy of the calling you have received" (Ephesians 4:1). He was not talking about their jobs. He encouraged them to adopt a lifestyle consistent with who they were in Christ. Calling in the Bible is one's position in Christ, not one's position in the world. Whatever you do, God calls you to live like a child of God and to bring honor to God through your actions. It matters less what you do *in* life than it does what you do *with* your life. For a believer, then, vocation, is what you do to provide for your needs in society, recognizing God's work in your life to lead you to that choice. Calling is a special mission in your life for God's purposes.

God calls people to join Him in reconciling the world to Himself. He uses what they do as a job to fulfill that calling. For example, Moses was a sheepherder; God called him to lead His people out of bondage. Peter was a fisherman; God called him to follow Jesus and become a fisher of men. Whether you are a postman or a preacher, God calls you to follow Him. God's call to follow Him has priority over your choice of careers. But whatever your career, God can use you to complete His plan for your life. Your task as a servant-minister to others is to discover how you can use your vocational skills for God's glory.

ENTHUSIASM

The word *enthusiasm* comes from a Greek word that literally means *in god*. The Greeks believed that a god could enter a person and inspire or enthuse him. Our word *enthusiasm* takes on the meaning *God in you*. Although the Greek word for *enthuse* is not found in the New Testament, the emphasis on God's presence, which energizes believers, is a recurring theme (see Matthew 28:18-20; John 14:20; 20:21-22; Acts 1:8). The Bible is clear that God's Holy Spirit is the source of passion for God's mission within believers. Paul declared that "Christ in you" is "the hope of glory" (Colossians 1:27). We do not generate hope on our own. God energizes us with His living Holy Spirit. Passion and enthusiasm for ministry come from God.

For Christian servants, enthusiasm is a God-given desire to serve Him by meeting the needs of others. Servants have a God-given passion to serve. A servant's greatest joy comes when he sees God at work, and he is part of it. Servanthood is a God-given passion for the success of God's plan.

Adapted from C. Gene Wilkes, *Jesus on Leadership* (Nashville: LifeWay Press, 1996), 35–82.

1. The sign gifts of tongues, interpretation of tongues, healing, and miracles are not included in this list.
2. Henry Blackaby, Richard Blackaby, and Claude King, *Experiencing God* (Nashville: LifeWay Press, 2007), 126.
3. Ken Voges and Ron Braund, *Understanding How Others Misunderstand You* (Chicago: Moody, 1990).

My SERVE Profile

Review the SERVE concepts on pages 101–3 and complete any of the inventories you wish to take that were referred to. Summarize what you have discovered by completing the following.

Believing that God has prepared me for servant ministry, I have discovered that He has molded me for service in the following ways.

God has given me these spiritual gifts: _____
_____

God has allowed these experiences to shape me for His purposes: _____
_____
_____
_____
_____
_____
_____

God has created me to relate naturally to others in this way: _____
_____
_____

God has given me opportunities to develop these vocational skills that can be used in His service:
_____
_____

God has burned in my heart the enthusiasm to serve in this area of ministry:
_____

I commit these gifts, talents, and abilities to God and His kingdom's service.

Signed _____ Date _____

C. Gene Wilkes, *Jesus on Leadership* (Nashville: LifeWay Press, 1996), 84.

Community Organizations and Agencies

Churches and individual believers can cooperate with community organizations as long as their purposes and values do not conflict with biblical truth. Use the following sources as a starting point for forming strategic alliances to meet community needs.

- Alcohol and drug rehabilitation programs
- Block organizations/neighborhood councils
- Chaplains
- Christian women's/mens job corps
- Church pastors/staff
- Civil/criminal court administrators
- Community-action programs
- Community centers
- Counseling services
- Crisis clinics
- Denominational organizations
- Denominational social-service agencies
- Disaster-relief organizations
- Employment office/manpower-training programs
- Food banks and pantries
- Goodwill Industries
- Habitat for Humanity
- Halfway houses/rescue missions
- Health agencies
- Head Start parent-group leaders
- Homes for mentally disabled persons
- Homes for unwed mothers
- Hospitals, hospital administrators/chaplains
- Housing-project managers/resident-council presidents
- Human-services departments
- Jail and prison administrators
- Low-income housing resident council members
- Mental-health departments
- Migrant ministry/migrant council
- Military-based commanders/chaplains
- Minority-group leaders
- Multihousing community managers
- Parent-teacher organizations
- Pregnancy resource center
- Prisons and jails
- Public-health departments
- Refugee-resettlement offices
- Salvation Army
- School principals, teachers, counselors
- Senior-adult centers and day care
- Shelters
- Social-service agency workers/directors
- Truant/probation/juvenile-delinquency officers
- Urban-renewal housing management/ low-income housing
- Visiting-nurses association
- Vocational-rehabilitation services
- Welfare department
- YMCA/YWCA

Adapted from *Adult Reading and Writing Literacy Missions Workshop Manual* (Alpharetta, GA: The North American Mission Board of the Southern Baptist Convention, 2007) and from *Community Assessment Manual*, *www.namb.net*, 11.

Discipleship Helps • *Minister to Others*

Kingdom-Coming Principles

As you read the following principles based on Luke 10:1-11, identify ways you can announce the coming of God's kingdom.

PREPARING

God equips you to go ahead of Him and prepare the way for His coming.

How are you preparing the way for Jesus to come into the lives of others?

_____

PARTICIPATING

Servants of God are participants in what God is doing.

How has God invited you to participate in His harvest lately?

_____

PRAYING

God leads people to pray about what He wants to do in answer to prayer.

How has becoming involved in ministry changed your prayer life?

_____

NETWORKING

Because God issues invitations to believers to join His work, those who participate with Him must be ready to do the same.

With whom have you networked lately to multiply your ministry?

_____

RELEASING

By releasing your resources, you provide someone an opportunity to participate in God's harvest.

As you have ministered to others, what resources has God called you to release?

_____

TRUSTING

Doing things God's way will require you to trust His way.

In what ways have you had to trust God while ministering to others?

_____

LEADING

Becoming a neighbor means meeting needs that others are not meeting.

Is your ministry meeting needs that others are not meeting? In what ways?

_____

INVITING

Ministry action is always a bridge to the gospel.

Describe an occasion when you successfully made the connection from ministry to the good news of Jesus. What was the result?

_____

Jesus' Model of Servant Leadership

Strive to follow Jesus' model of servant leadership. Here are some characteristics of His relationship with His disciples that demonstrate servant leadership.

○ Modeled an abiding relationship with the Father
○ Prayed and followed the Father's directions
○ Emphasized Kingdom values and purposes
○ Practiced sacrifice and service
○ Demonstrated authenticity and integrity
○ Lived with intentionality 24/7
○ Learned from testing and refinement in the crucible of life
○ Called the disciples to Kingdom service
○ Set the pace and called the disciples to imitate Him
○ Took opportunities for teachable moments
○ Allowed failure without rejection but with purpose
○ Showed patience
○ Valued the disciples
○ Held the disciples accountable
○ Celebrated and encouraged the disciples
○ Used stories to communicate truth

Go back and place a check mark beside qualities you already demonstrate as you model a servant lifestyle for others.

What are three qualities do you need to work on?

1. _____

2. _____

3. _____

Leader Guide

If you have not read the introduction beginning on page 5, do so before continuing.

First Peter 4:10 instructs, "Based on the gift they have received, everyone should use it to serve others, as good managers of the varied grace of God." God calls all believers to use the gifts He has given us to serve others—to minister sacrificially and compassionately in ways that draw unsaved people to Christ. By making servanthood a lifestyle, we will have multiple opportunities to develop relationships, meet needs, and share the good news of salvation in Jesus Christ. *Minister to Others* teaches Christians important biblical principles for living a life of service to others for God's glory.

SMALL-GROUP STUDY

Minister to Others is a six-session study designed for both individual and small-group study. Each week participants will study five daily lessons that introduce principles for developing and expressing a servant lifestyle. Then they will attend a weekly group session to discuss what they have learned and ways they have practiced ministry during the week. In a small group of other believers, Christians can learn from one another, encourage and strengthen one another, and minister to one another. The body of Christ can function best as members assume responsibility for helping one another grow in Christlikeness. Encourage participants to study the book during the week and then join others in a

small group to process and apply what they have learned.

This study was designed to create learning experiences by doing. The daily lessons and weekly group sessions strongly encourage participants to immediately begin practicing ministry to others as they discover new ideas for doing so.

Provide a separate group for every 8 to 12 participants so that everyone will be able to participate actively.

A guide for each small-group session appears at the end of each week's daily devotionals.

ONE-TO-ONE MENTORING

If circumstances prevent your studying this book in a small-group setting, you may choose to use a one-to-one mentoring or coaching process. To do so, study the devotionals each day and meet at least once each week to discuss what you are learning and experiencing. Use the session plan at the end of each week's devotionals to get ideas for your personal discussions and prayer time. Pray for and encourage each other by phone.

If you serve as the mentor, study the entire book in advance so that you will be able to walk another individual through the process, asking questions to facilitate his or her study of the book. Your role in holding the person accountable and helping them process and practice what they are learning will be invaluable.

ENLISTING PARTICIPANTS

Any believer who wants to obey Jesus' Great Commission will benefit from this study. It is especially designed, however, for individuals who want to develop a servant lifestyle or engage in ministry as a means of building relational bridges by which they will intentionally share the gospel. As you enlist participants, give them a book and ask them to study the introduction and week 1 before the first group session. Include mature believers in the group so that any subgroups you form will include someone who is comfortable leading discussions and praying for others.

ORDERING BOOKS

Each participant will need a copy of this book. To order, write to LifeWay Church Resources Customer Service; One LifeWay Plaza; Nashville, TN 37234-0113; fax order to (615) 251-5933; phone toll free (800) 458-2772; order online at *www.lifeway.com;* e-mail *orderentry@lifeway.com;* or visit a LifeWay Christian Store.

SELECTING A LEADER

The leader of the small-group study should be someone who personally practices a servant lifestyle and who uses ministry opportunities to lead people to Christ. From a practical standpoint, the leader will serve as a coach to the individuals in the small group; but the leader must also actively practice a servant lifestyle so that he or she can answer participants' questions and share wisdom and practical ideas that come from personal experience.

YOUR ROLE AS THE LEADER

You are not required to be a content expert to teach this course. Participants study the content during the week. Your role is to facilitate group discussion, sharing, and praying to process and apply the ministry principles that participants have learned and practiced during the week. Be sensitive to the spiritual growth of members and pay special attention to those who may struggle along the way. Believers who are unaccustomed to ministering and witnessing might find themselves outside their comfort zones. Don't force participants to do something they are not ready for. However, gently nudge them toward active ministry by presenting the biblical mandate, being a good example, and pointing them to God's spiritual provision for the task.

TIME AND SCHEDULE

This course is designed for six sessions. The group sessions need to follow the study of the week's daily devotions. Members will need to have books in advance so that they can study the first week's material before the first session. Allow at least 60 minutes for each session. Some groups may prefer longer sessions to accommodate more sharing, discussion, and prayer time.

You may prefer to start with an introductory session so that you can overview the study, distribute books, get acquainted, and make assignments for the first week. This will add one additional session to the study.

PREPARING FOR THE STUDY

Make prayer a major part of your preparation throughout the course. God will work and guide in answer to prayer. Leading the small-group sessions should not require large amounts of time in advance preparation. Each week study the suggestions that follow the week's devotionals. Use these as options, not as a rigid structure to follow. Allow your group's needs and ministry involvement to dictate the way you use your discussion and prayer time each week. Decide which activities and questions to use in your study and determine approximate times for transitions between segments. Select activities that are most appropriate for your group's maturity level.

DURING THE SESSION

1. *Opening prayer.* Start each group time with prayer. It may be helpful to begin with a time of silence to allow the group to focus their minds and hearts on the Lord. Then you or someone in the group can voice a prayer asking for the Spirit's guidance during your time together.

2. *Learning goals.* State the learning goals to set the direction for the group session.

3. *Reviewing this week's material.* These activities help the group review the ministry principles members have studied during the week. Invite responses to the questions and activities.

4. *Ministering to others.* This section allows participants to share ministry they have engaged in during the week and challenges them to further action. Watch for ways to encourage participants to increase their sensitivity to ministry opportunities, to cultivate relationships, to connect with other ministry partners, and to follow through with a gospel witness.

5. *Praying together.* Members will pray in pairs or as a group for the specific ministry needs that have been discussed during the session and for God to equip them to minister.

6. *Previewing the next week.* Use the introductory page for the next week to give a quick overview of the upcoming study. You could invite volunteers to prepare in advance to introduce the next week's topic.

This guide may help you lead your group, but the Holy Spirit is your true Guide. Allow Him to show you what questions to ask and the direction He wants the group to go each week.

Two Ways to Earn Credit
for Studying LifeWay Christian Resources Material

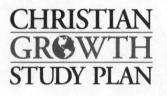

CHRISTIAN GROWTH STUDY PLAN

CONTACT INFORMATION:
Christian Growth Study Plan
One LifeWay Plaza, MSN 117
Nashville, TN 37234
CGSP info line 1-800-968-5519
www.lifeway.com/CGSP
To order resources 1-800-458-2772

Christian Growth Study Plan resources are available for course credit for personal growth and church leadership training.

Courses are designed as plans for personal spiritual growth and for training current and future church leaders. To receive credit, complete the book, material, or activity. Respond to the learning activities or attend group sessions, when applicable, and show your work to your pastor, staff member, or church leader. Then go to *www.lifeway.com/CGSP*, or call the toll-free number for instructions for receiving credit and your certificate of completion.

For information about studies in the Christian Growth Study Plan, refer to the current catalog online at the CGSP Web address. This program and certificate are free LifeWay services to you.

Need a CEU?

CONTACT INFORMATION:
CEU Coordinator
One LifeWay Plaza, MSN 150
Nashville, TN 37234
Info line 1-800-968-5519
www.lifeway.com/CEU

Receive Continuing Education Units (CEUs) when you complete group Bible studies by your favorite LifeWay authors.

Some studies are approved by the Association of Christian Schools International (ACSI) for CEU credits. Do you need to renew your Christian school teaching certificate? Gather a group of teachers or neighbors and complete one of the approved studies. Then go to *www.lifeway.com/CEU* to submit a request form or to find a list of ACSI-approved LifeWay studies and conferences. Book studies must be completed in a group setting. Online courses approved for ACSI credit are also noted on the course list. The administrative cost of each CEU certificate is only $10 per course.

The Growing Disciples Series

New and growing believers need a firm foundation on which to build their lives. The Growing Disciples Series provides short-term Bible studies that establish a strong foundation for a life of following Jesus Christ. The series begins with *The Call to Follow Christ*, which introduces six spiritual disciplines. Subsequent studies help believers understand and practice disciplines that strengthen their love relationship with Christ and develop a lifestyle of faithful, fruitful obedience. Watch for the following six-week resources as the series grows:

Growing Disciples: Abide in Christ
Growing Disciples: Live in the Word
Growing Disciples: Pray in Faith
Growing Disciples: Fellowship with Believers
Growing Disciples: Witness to the World
Growing Disciples: Minister to Others

For a free 20-minute Webinar on the series, go to *http://lifeway.acrobat.com/growingdisciples*.

The Call to Follow Christ: Six Disciplines for New and Growing Believers by Claude King is a seven-session, foundational resource that introduces the six disciplines in the series. This unique workbook includes a music CD with seven songs sung by Dámaris Carbaugh that will enrich participants' daily 10- to 15-minute interactive devotion/study time. Item 001303666

To order these resources and to check availability, fax (615) 251-5933; phone toll free (800) 458-2772; order online at *www.lifeway.com;* e-mail *orderentry@lifeway.com;* visit the LifeWay Christian Store serving you; or write to LifeWay Church Resources Customer Service; One LifeWay Plaza; Nashville, TN 37234-0113.